WHERE FAITH AND ECONOMICS MEET

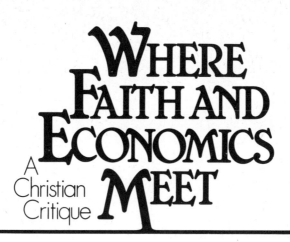

WHERE FAITH AND ECONOMICS MEET

A Christian Critique

David M. Beckmann

AUGSBURG Publishing House • Minneapolis

WHERE FAITH AND ECONOMICS MEET

To Janet,
of course

Contents

1

A Holy Materialism?

This book is like a letter home—one of those rare letters in which a person needs to share life-changing truths growing out of new experiences.

I am both a Christian pastor and a World Bank economist. During the past ten years I have lived at various times in Bangladesh, Ghana, England, and the United States, and have traveled to nearly sixty countries on five continents. I started writing this book because of my own need to make coherent sense of my perspective as an economist, my exposure to different countries, and my Christian faith.

I trust the effort will prove helpful to others, by placing personal life-style decisions in the context of world issues and economic concerns in the context of religious faith.

During the present period of world economic difficulties, it would be appropriate for us to reflect, not only on short-term adjustments for coping with higher energy costs and inflation, but also on our long-term goals as individuals and societies. We could even take the world's current economic malaise as a warning. The modern world is too often characterized by frantic consumerism, arrogant planning, sophisticated means to irrational ends, and social injustice. Such a world is vulnerable, not only to short-term disturbances, but also to long-term disaster.

Might it be possible to consecrate modern economic life? The phrase "holy materialism" seems paradoxical, to some people even offensive. I do not introduce it to suggest that crass consumerism may not be so bad after all, nor to recommend a view of history which considers ideas uninfluential. Rather, I have used it as the title for this introduction, because it juxtaposes two aspects of life which should be integrated, but seldom are: religion and economics.

THE NEED FOR A COHERENT VISION

Most of us tend to compartmentalize life. We manage our economic affairs as if religion were something entirely separate and unrelated. Few of us make connections between our private economic affairs or faith and the national and international economic issues we read about. It is as if private economic affairs, religious faith, and broader economic issues could be put in three separate boxes:

```
┌──────────────┐   ┌──────────────┐   ┌──────────────┐
│              │   │              │   │              │
│   Private    │   │              │   │   Broader    │
│  economic    │   │  Religious   │   │  economic    │
│  affairs     │   │    faith     │   │   issues     │
│              │   │              │   │              │
└──────────────┘   └──────────────┘   └──────────────┘
```

In fact, many important decisions cannot be fitted into just one box:

• A student looks into the future. What sort of career should she pursue? Should she aim for the affluence her parents achieved, or choose a more modest, committed lifestyle? These are personal economic decisions; but they will be influenced by the student's sensitivity to social problems, and they have a religious dimension.

• Two political candidates offer a clear choice. The incumbent has consistently voted for legislation intended to benefit the poor. His opponent says his top priority is lower taxes, arguing that welfare programs are wasteful and ineffective anyway. The voters' choice is economic: it will make a difference to public policy and to their own after-tax incomes. It is also a religious decision.

• A Tanzanian pastor visiting the United States is invited to address a church in Indianapolis about Christian mission in Africa. His audience is surprised when he talks instead on two political topics: South Africa and the New International Economic Order. He says that a major part of foreign missionary work for U.S. Christians is to change U.S. foreign policy. He suggests that his audience contribute time and money to lobby for a particular bill being considered in Congress. His speech is surprising, because he has refused to accept the segregation of private business, Christian faith, and politics into separate boxes.

• A World Bank economist is formulating recommendations which, if approved by his management, will be conveyed to the government of a developing country. He has before him a mass of data and the results of a computerized model of this particular economy. But how, in the end, does he focus on key suggestions? His judgment is guided by moral, as well as technical, considerations. Even if he doesn't spell them out explicitly, his recommendations may well have cultural or religious implications in the country concerned.

The diagram below represents a more realistic approach than the three separate boxes. Analyzing such relationships

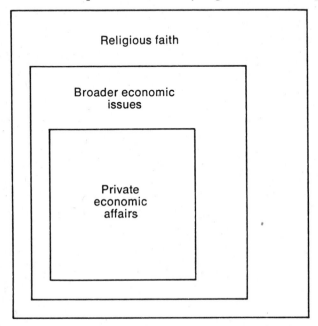

may stretch the mind. But it is intrinsically satisfying to have some understanding, however tentative, of how our working and spending are related to God and to the concerns of people in Yugoslavia or Bangladesh. Recognizing these relationships is a way of praising God. Not recognizing them is morally irresponsible, because our decisions about work, spending, and voting *do* affect people far away.

Many traditional societies enjoyed a holistic vision of the meaning of life. But the vaulting complexities of modern economics have, for the most part, broken loose from simpler, ancient wisdoms. Economic development often rushes forward according to its own mechanical dynamic—competitive, technical, and vast in scale.[1] The saints and heroes who capture the modern religious imagination—people like Martin Luther King, Mahatma Gandhi, Mother Teresa, Dom Helder Camara, and Julius Nyerere—are often distinguished by their gift for reintegrating secular forces into a spiritual vision.

There is, among Christians, an earnest minority who are trying to reorder their life-styles and politics to make them congruent with their faith and their understanding of broad economic issues. There are leaders in all parts of the Christian church who are helping members deal with world economic issues, relate them to their faith, and take specific actions to change things for the better.

• The Roman Catholic Church has addressed economic and social issues in a fresh way since the Second Vatican Council.[2] It has been shifting its political allegiances, no longer so often buttressing the status quo, more often siding with the poor against the rich.[3] The journeys of Pope John Paul II have personalized the Roman Catholic Church's concern about the economic and social realities of the Communist countries (in his own Poland), the wealthy capitalist countries (in the United States), and the developing countries (in Latin America, the Middle East, and Africa). When the Pope visited the United States, the temptations of wealth and the need for international sharing were among his major themes.

• Leaders of the more liberal, ecumenical Protestant churches have long been critical of domestic and international injustices. Meetings and publications sponsored by the World Council of Churches have been especially open to counter-establishment ideas and, increasingly, to viewpoints from the developing countries.[4]

• Recently, some conservative evangelical Protestants have begun to address economic and social questions critically, too. Concern about world hunger and a growing interest in simpler life-styles have taken root among some theologically conservative Protestants. Books like Jim Wallis' *Agenda for Biblical People* and Ron Sider's *Rich Christians in an Age of Hunger* address personal and political economic questions with fresh and uncompromising spiritual vigor.[5]

This present book is a contribution to these movements in the churches. It has three characteristics which should make it helpful:

• It offers a *broad* perspective. It is tempting to focus too narrowly on the here and now, rather than working toward an overview of our role in economic history and the worldwide economy. We might, as a result, overemphasize relatively simple life-style gestures (eating less meat, for example) and neglect more costly, significant changes (career choices, for example). We might latch onto current waves of moral concern without much understanding of long-term underlying issues.

• I have attempted to provide a *balanced* view. It is tempting to accept someone else's prescriptions for how we ought to eat and live or how we ought to think and vote. But fundamentally like-minded people will sometimes come to different conclusions if they are thinking independently about complex matters. I have presented both sides of several controversies, not hiding my own opinions, but concentrating on basic moral values.

• This book is *seriously theological*. Some Christian books on economics just discuss current events from a moral standpoint, perhaps pointing to analogous situations in the Bible. In this book I suggest a conceptual framework which may help to put economics in theological context. The Aim is to root our economic life in the character of God, to relate mundane tasks and technical debates to him, and to open up possibilities for consecrating economic life —for a "holy materialism."

ECONOMIC CULTURE

Where do faith and economics meet? In *economic culture*. By *economic culture* I mean modern materialistic culture, forged during the Industrial Revolution and the Enlightenment, and now the most powerful and universal cultural influence in the world.

The fundamental insight of this book, which for me grounds economics in theology, is that *the values of economic culture have been shaped by the Lord and reflect, although only in distorted and broken ways, his own character.*

This insight into the relationship between economic culture and its Christian roots can, first, clarify the vague dissatisfaction with affluence which many people feel and help identify reforms we ought to make for the sake of a stable and satisfying prosperity. Second, it can give balance and theological perspective to our attitudes toward the basic issues which repeatedly resurface in domestic debates and international confrontation between the political Left and Right. Third, it has implications for the relationships between rich and poor nations and between religion and economic development.

Finally, this insight may change our attitudes toward the ordinary stuff of life: the routines of a job, watching the evening news, grocery shopping, or mowing the lawn on a weekend. God is present in our affluence and in the habits which maintain it. His Word is like leaven in the world, raising not only the spirits of humanity, but also our material prosperity.

We might even come to see all production and consumption, as well as the bread and wine on the altar, as something God can make holy. He takes our bread and wine, fruits of the earth and human labor, and gives them back as Christ among us.[6]

In the chapters which follow, I will first describe what I have chosen to call *economic culture* and highlight its role as an engine for economic growth (Chapter 2). Then I will critique the values of economic culture in light of Christian values, suggesting how the divorce of economic culture from God has resulted in a twisted, often self-frustrating affluence (Chapter 3).

Chapters 4, 5, and 6 use the book's basic concepts— economic culture and its relation to Christian faith—to probe the two great economic divisions of the modern world.

1. Value conflicts within economic culture contribute to *the division of the modern world between capitalist and socialist tendencies.* Is there a Christian perspective on the debate between Right and Left?

2. Value conflicts, both within economic culture and between it and traditional culture, also complicate *the division of the modern world between rich and poor.* Does a Christian critique of economic culture suggest any fruitful approaches to the problem of world poverty?

Finally, although most of this book is about Christian morality, Christianity is more than morality. Christianity is centered in faith that God is for us despite our immorality. Does faith in God's grace have any relationship to economics? In Chapter 7, I will suggest that Christian faith can be the vital core and motivation for a holy materialism.

2

Modern Prosperity and the Values That Shape Us

In comparing ourselves to friends who have even more, we sometimes forget how affluent we are. Anyone who has lived in Asia, Africa, or Latin America, however, knows that most people in the United States never really need anything. There are extremely poor people in the United States too, but most of us have no idea what it means to need food for the family or clean water to drink. We wear clothes more for decoration than for protection. I remember trying to explain to friends in Bangladesh—people for whom bicycles are luxuries—how it could be that some people in the United States who own cars consider themselves poor.

AN END TO ECONOMIC GROWTH?

We live in a rich country, but during the last generation the world as a whole has grown more prosperous than ever before. Even in Bangladesh, despite the disasters and wars of recent years, fewer babies die, common people know much more of the wider world, and mass deaths from famine are less likely than they were three or four decades ago.

The economies of the rich capitalist countries—mainly North America and Western Europe—have been growing steadily for two to three hundred years. Between about 1950 and 1975 their economies expanded more rapidly than ever before. The Communist bloc countries grew as fast, or slightly faster, than North America and Western Europe over this period. On the average economies of the less-developed countries of Asia, Africa, and Latin America also grew as quickly as those of the rich capitalist countries, certainly more quickly than ever before in history.[1] Some newly industrialized countries grew at unprecedented rates, and during the late 1970s, although economic growth has slowed for most of the world, some oil-producing developing nations have benefited greatly.

The world's economic expansion over the last generation has not benefited poor people as much as it might have. Much of the production increase of the developing countries was eaten up—almost literally—by population increases. The survival of so many children who would have died a generation ago is a tremendous gain, but production growth has had to be shared among growing populations.

In addition, poor people have suffered from a generally inequitable distribution of the benefits of growth. Within developing countries poor people have almost consistently benefited less from development than relatively well-off people, and many of the poorest of the developing countries have enjoyed very little economic growth. Very poor people in some parts of South Asia and Latin America may actually have less than they did a generation ago.

In general, however, the unprecedented growth of the last generation has also improved conditions somewhat even for the very poor in poor societies:

• A generation ago perhaps a third of all adults in developing countries could read; now about half can read. The proportion of children in primary school has risen almost everywhere, and the proportion in secondary school has doubled.

• In the past two or three decades the developing countries have registered increases in life expectancy that took the developed countries a century to achieve. Infant mortality is down, and several killer diseases are under control. Increases in life expectancy suggest widely shared improvements in standards of living.[2]

Is the long period of economic growth which gave rise to these basic gains, as well as the affluence of the richer countries, now over? A number of social critics and ethicists are telling us that resource shortages signal an end to growth, and worldwide "stagflation" adds to the pessimism. Some of the critics argue that economic growth *shouldn't* continue, that saner, less materialistic lifestyles would imply less growth, and that the world should concentrate on meeting the basic needs of the poor instead of on more economic growth.[3]

No return to the boom times of the 1950s and 1960s is in sight, but I don't agree that the long climb to world affluence since the Industrial Revolution is or should be coming to an end:

• **Resources.** During the last generation of rapid economic growth, energy was cheap and little attention was paid to the environmental side effects of growth. As E. F. Schumacher pointed out in *Small Is Beautiful,* we were treating the exploitation of natural resources just like other income, whereas in fact we were spending our natural capital.[4] The negative environmental effects of growth accumulated more and more rapidly, however, until by the early 1970s they were impossible to ignore. Then, at the end of 1973, came the first stunning increase in oil prices.

OPEC (Organization of Petroleum Exporting Countries) succeeded in establishing monopoly prices, and, more important, demonstrating that producer nations were now fully in control of their own resources (that the United States would no longer send in Marines or the CIA). Perhaps even more important for the long term, OPEC's action called attention to the increasing scarcity of fossil fuels and the eventual depletion of other mineral resources, too.

We are in a period of costly adjustment to environmental awareness and higher-priced energy. Businesses complain about poorly-designed and shifting government regulations intended to protect the environment, but even well-designed and stable regulations will imply real costs to the economy—costs we used to pay by breathing foul air and losing natural beauties. People complain about higher prices for gasoline, but, in fact, oil prices in the United States are still being held below world-market levels, and natural gas prices are set on the basis of production cost rather than scarcity value. Most analysts agree that oil and natural gas prices should be allowed to double or triple to encourage serious conservation and the development of solar energy and other renewable energy sources.[5]

Over the next decade we will be paying dearly for adjustment—insulating homes, densifying cities, reorienting the automobile industry, and redesigning factories. We will be paying for a better environment, too, continuing with cleanup jobs on polluted rivers and city air, as well as insisting that the environmental costs of new projects (including possible energy projects like strip mining and nuclear energy) be taken into account. The changes in technology and life-style will be substantial. We will never again enjoy the "subsidies" provided by ignorable environmental side effects and apparently undepletable natural resources.

The long-term cost will be huge, but not unsustainable.

To get some idea of the orders of magnitude involved, figure that primary energy costs are about 5% of U.S. GNP (Gross National Product). If average primary-energy costs were to double again in real terms by the end of the century, and energy use were to grow in proportion to GNP, then U.S. GNP in the year 2000 would be only about 5% less than it would have been otherwise. This would be equivalent to a loss of only 0.4% per year, compared to average growth rates for the U.S. of 4.3% per year in the 1960s or 2.8% per year in the 1970s.[6] Even a 2% annual growth rate, although low by recent standards, would be about equal to the historical average for Europe and North America since the Industrial Revolution and would imply a doubling of output every generation.

• **Stagflation.** Slack demand in the world economy is primarily due to the restrictive policies of major governments in their efforts to curb chronic inflation. Virtually the entire world has experienced persistent and climbing inflation since the end of the Second World War, but OPEC price rises in 1973-75, by adding several percentage points to inflation already running at about 6% in the United States, shocked the world into placing a much higher priority on stable prices.

With hindsight we can see the main cause of chronic inflation was the misuse of "Keynesian" economics. A little inflation could "heat up" an economy, reducing unemployment and speeding growth. Economists and politicians who had been through the Depression were willing to allow creeping inflation in order to keep unemployment at an absolute minimum.

With time, however, it became clear that only unanticipated inflation does the trick, in effect by fooling workers into taking jobs which seem to offer higher wages than they do. When inflation becomes widely anticipated, it is no longer as effective in keeping unemployment down. Inflation becomes much more difficult to control then, too, because workers and firms insist on higher and higher wages and prices in accordance with their expectations for inflation. Our economy is now dominated by big government, big unions, and big corporations, in which rising wages and prices are somewhat insulated from the price discipline of free-market competition.

There are a number of specific measures which can be taken to bring inflation down again—stimulating investment and productivity, breaking up monopolies (also the monopolies of unions or governments) to encourage price competition, and coping with unemployment through programs (training, public jobs) targeted at groups who have the most trouble getting employed rather than by heating up the entire economy. In addition, however, governments and central banks will have to exercise general restraint in macroeconomic management—letting economies cool down again through slack demand and relatively high unemployment until people come to expect stable prices.

For this reason, as well as because of resource scarcities, the 1980s, like the 1970s, are likely to be a period of slow growth compared to the boom times of the 1950s and 1960s. But although the "stagflation" we are now suffering is a complex and difficult problem, it is not so much different from ordinary recession. With proper economic management, there is no reason the world should not return to better times after some years of restraint.

• **Shift in Values.** The counterculture of protest and anti-materialism in the 1960s may have pioneered a popular shift in values, away from a fascination with GNP and higher money incomes, toward satisfactions which money cannot buy. The slowdown in economic growth in the 1970s has inspired much more widespread reflection on the consumerism of the past decades. Many families are making a virtue of their necessity to cut back.

This is a welcome trend. It may be more wholesome for many of us to eat less and turn the thermostat down.

If values are shifting, however, it would imply a redefinition of growth, not an abandonment of the deep social dynamic which has sustained gradual economic growth over the last two centuries. Most economists would agree that, precisely speaking, economic growth should be defined as a shift to a higher level of "welfare," that is, an expansion in the range of choice; growth in GNP (the value of what is bought and sold) is simply a more easily measurable proxy. If a man chooses not to work Christmas Eve in order to spend the holiday with his family, his money income and the GNP may be slightly lower, but the man and his family will obviously be better off. If GNP were to stabilize or fall because of a shift in preferences toward nonmonetary goods (e.g. more family-oriented leisure time), that might well represent a higher level of welfare. If economic growth is defined in this way, learning more satisfying preferences should be considered an *increase* in economic growth.

• **Mass Poverty.** About 800 million people in the world still live in absolute poverty, their basic needs for food, shelter, health, and education unmet.[7] Some analysts have recommended that the world should not be so preoccupied with economic growth, but should concentrate on meeting the basic needs of the poor. Again, the problem is that GNP is not an adequate measure of welfare. An extra dollar to a poor family may be the equivalent of two or three more dollars to a well-off family. But to aim more directly for increases in the incomes of the poor (growth with justice) would not be to abandon the historical project of expanding the range of human choice. It is unlikely that the basic needs of the world's poorest people will ever be met without sustained economic growth for the nations of South Asia and Africa where most of them live, and the growth of those nations has been closely correlated to the growth of the world economy as a whole.

In conclusion, then, the world has experienced an un- precedented expansion in the range of human choice over the last two centuries. So far this growth has been concen- trated primarily in Europe and among descendants of Europeans in the Americas and elsewhere, but most of the rest of the world is developing now, too. Problems like oil scarcity and the persistence of mass poverty will require substantial changes in the character and direction of eco- nomic growth, but economic growth itself need not come to an end. The present era of economic growth probably will not last forever, but the end is not yet in sight.

VALUES CONDUCIVE TO GROWTH

What has caused the unprecedented and resilient eco- nomic growth which characterizes the present era? One important cause has been that modern culture is conducive to economic growth.[8]

When we read about people in history or meet people from other parts of the world, we become aware that we have a particular culture. Our ways of dressing, eating, talking, thinking, and praying are distinctive. Our society has trained us to value certain things more than others. Unless we are confronted by people from other times and places, we may not even be aware of the cultural assump- tions we have been taught. They seem natural and inevi- table. Like fish in water, we are unaware of how life as we know it depends on the culture around us.

To become aware of our culture is to become critical of it. Is our society right in what it values, or should we, as individuals and as a society, behave differently? A sense of our culture's evolution may spark within us the courage and imagination to *reshape*—not only to be *shaped by*—our strand of history.

The dominant culture of our time might be called *economic culture,* because it is particularly suited to economic growth. More often it is simply called modern culture, because its ideals have been so influential during the last 200 years.

Modern *economic culture* began to emerge in Europe about the time of the Renaissance and Reformation. The values which constitute economic culture were not altogether new to the world. They had long been part of European culture, and some of them were prevalent in other cultures, too. But they came together in a distinctive way in modern Europe, taking clear shape by the close of the eighteenth century—the time of the Industrial Revolution, the American Revolution, and the French Revolution. Modern values were thoroughly integrated into personal behavior and social institutions first in England, the leading nation of the Industrial Revolution. They were probably most clearly expressed during the French Enlightenment and French Revolution, however. Because French society was relatively archaic and rigid in comparison to England, French thinkers mounted an intellectual crusade for modernization.[9]

We might take six Enlightenment ideals as being representative of modern, economic culture:

this-worldliness

progress

reason

liberty

equality

fraternity

These six values and the ways they foster economic growth are the subject of the rest of this chapter. In discussing what these ideals mean and how they contribute to growth, I will use some contemporary examples, because these values often shape our personal behavior and social institutions in rich countries like the United States. I will also draw examples from history and from the current experience of developing countries, because the revolutionary implications of these values are most obvious in situations where they are set against other "pre-modern" cultures. As the discussion ranges from one country to another, one century to another, a few examples may not ring true to a particular reader's experience or knowledge of history. I have done my best to be accurate in detail, but, in any case, what is important to the argument is the overall credibility of the thesis that these modern values are a factor contributing to growth.

Modern values have spread around the globe with stunning speed, partly because of their association with economic growth. England and France were the early leaders in modernization, but nascent German nationalism rallied around modern values, too. The United States had few fixed traditions and so was able to seize on modern values with unique single-mindedness. A key factor behind the rapid pace and relatively painless character of U.S. economic development was, in the words of historians John A. Garraty and Peter Gay, "the American ethos, which gave unreserved sanction to all behavior conducive to economic growth." [10]

"Enlightened" nations have tended to advance economically and thus gain the military clout to impose Enlightenment values on other peoples (Napoleon's armies in Europe and, later, European colonial armies throughout the rest of the world). The wave of nationalistic revolutions which has swept the world during the last two centuries has reasserted the independence of economically backward peoples. Nationalistic revolutionaries, however, have generally imposed modernization on their own peoples, in part because modernization and economic growth seemed crucial for regaining military parity and political independence.[11]

The widespread acceptance of economic values is not proof of their ethical reliability. An Indian friend, rightly appreciative of India's rich and ancient culture, reminded me wryly that "barbarians" have been militarily powerful before, and that Coca-Cola is just as widespread as the supposedly loftier aspects of economic culture. Whether base or lofty, however, Enlightenment values are today advocated by virtually all the governments of the world, often contradicting some of the traditional values of their own peoples. Economic culture has become the most universal culture in history. A Thai schoolboy or a Kenyan politician is nearly as likely to espouse faith in progress, for example, as a businessman in New York or a commissar in Moscow.

These six values are so basic to our society that they are no longer ideas which we have; they have us.[12] We assume *this world* is important, and we enjoy material prosperity. Almost all of us aim for personal *progress*—working toward the job, the family situation, and the comforts we think we would enjoy five or ten years from now. We think social progress is possible—that poverty, for example, is a problem to be solved rather than a mystery to be endured, as other cultures have assumed.

We are *rational*, or at least pretend to be. When I lived in Ghana I was often struck by my own automatic rationalism. I remember when a church building partly collapsed; several Ghanaian friends were filled with awe, wondering at the spiritual significance of the calamity. I doubted there was any spiritual significance at all, attributing the collapse to faulty construction and poor maintenance.

The ideals of *liberty, equality,* and *fraternity* seem right and natural to us as norms for modern society. For example, in my work at the World Bank I can argue that some aspect of a housing project is valuable because it will lead to a more equitable distribution of income (*equality*) or more cohesive neighborhoods (*fraternity*), but it would be considered silly to suggest that the Bank should finance a component to deepen prayer life. The value assumptions on which modern, secular institutions like the World Bank are based rule out certain kinds of involvements which might have seemed appropriate for public institutions in pre-modern times.

Let us now look at how each of these six values emerged and how they contribute to economic growth.

This-worldliness. *This-worldliness* is the presupposition of modern culture. This world of delight and decay is valuable. Work is worth doing, not demeaning. Earthly pleasures are to be enjoyed, not avoided as sin. Modern this-worldliness is in sharp contrast to the other-worldliness of some other cultures—their preoccupation with invisible realities, their communication with spirits, and their mortification of earthly desire.

Modern prosperity depends on the grocer who cares about crisp lettuce, either for his customers' sake or because a little extra income is important to him. The pleasant homes in which we live depend on men and women who enjoy them enough to invest hard-earned money in soft carpeting, who subject themselves to the never-ending labor of cleaning and maintenance, and who spend some of their holidays redecorating. On a grander scale, we would not have the Brandenburg concertos if Bach had not considered musical pleasure worthy of genius and dedication, or if there had not been a long tradition of musical achievement leading up to Bach.

In European history, the things of this world took on new importance during the Renaissance and Reformation. The Renaissance revived the this-worldliness of the classics, holding it together with Christianity in a cultured and aristocratic synthesis. The Reformation, meanwhile, brought people's attention down to earth with all the dynamism and mass appeal of religious passion. Rather than simply making space for mundane life by placing spiritual concerns to one side, the Reformation emptied the monasteries of northern Europe and sent the pious into secular vocations with monkish dedication. The Reformers taught that salvation was not to be earned by repeating the mass, nor in cloistered devotion, but was free for all through faith in Jesus Christ; some of the careers and money which had been invested in elaborate churches and monasteries could now be turned to secular purposes.

With a new awareness of the importance of this world, Christendom began to reform itself, so that its earthly life would better reflect its spiritual ideals. Both the Protestant Reformation and Roman Catholic Counter-Reformation made radical changes, not only in doctrine, but also in the practice of religion and the organization of society. It was Puritans—radical Protestants—who eventually led the political and industrial revolutions of Britain, and the Counter-Reformation flowered in the cultural refinement of France under Louis XIV.

Progress. People learned to believe in *progress* from the sixteenth century onward as Europeans, in fact, achieved progress on almost all fronts. Economic production went up, inventions were made, scientific knowledge expanded, democratic government appeared, and European manners became more cultivated. By the middle of the eighteenth century Turgot, a French philosopher lecturing at the Sorbonne on "The Successive Advances of the Human Mind," could claim:

> The human race, viewed from its earliest beginning, presents itself to the eye of the philosopher as a vast whole which, like every individual being, has its time

of childhood and progress. . . . Manners become gentler; the mind becomes enlightened; nations, hitherto living in isolation, draw nearer to one another; trade and political relations link up the various quarters of the globe; and the whole body of mankind, through vicissitudes of calm and tempest, of fair days and foul, continues its onward march, albeit with tardy steps, toward an ever-nearing perfection.[13]

Such optimism became more and more widespread during the nineteenth century, even while the foundations of Europe began to shake. Industrialization was creating foul, crowded cities and the increasing class conflict which Marx analyzed. Freud discovered how potent primitive urges had remained. Darwin's theory stressed kinship with the animals. The general expansion of knowledge seemed to leave less and less sphere for the workings of God.

In the twentieth century the belief in progress has been further assaulted by the Depression and cataclysmic wars. Developments in art, literature, and philosophy have been more often disturbing or depressing than encouraging. The idea of progress does survive, however. Most of us still behave as if we believe we are able to make things at least a little better. We still tend to hope for universal progress, even if we are painfully aware of the likelihood of more war and devastation.

Some sort of *belief* in progress is, in fact, virtually a prerequisite for *attaining* progress. In Bangladesh I once organized several farmers' tours of the various development agencies and demonstration farms in our area. At the end of each two-day tour, we sat down on the grass, and I asked each man what ideas he had learned that he was willing to try. The relatively wealthy and educated farmers had all taken advantage of the opportunity. One rich farmer had bought an improved plow, and a high school teacher who also owned a farm had a whole notebook full of ideas he wanted to try. When I asked really poor farmers, however, how they planned to change, they looked at me blankly. In almost each instance a relatively wealthy farmer took the initiative, perhaps telling his poorer neighbor: "You should plant mulberry trees around your house and take up sericulture," or "You could at least put into practice some of the hygiene information we learned at the clinic." The poor man would agree submissively.

After two tours I began to realize just how few of the development ideas being offered were useful to the very poor. They couldn't afford a plow that would cut deeper, and their work animals were too sickly to pull it anyway. They couldn't read or write, so how could they record and reflect on new ideas? In addition to those handicaps, however, I suspect the poorer farmers were simply not in the habit of envisioning themselves in improved situations. Crushing poverty and ignorance had taught them not to expect progress.

Within the developed countries, too, people who are better able to envision the future they want, setting specific goals and timetables, are most likely to succeed. It often works at the societal level as well. Because people 25 years ago had grand visions of overcoming racism, and because of all the legal actions, marches, and ambitious programs that dream inspired, small, but significant gains have been made.

Reason. The use of applied *reason* to produce wealth commands almost universal respect. The conquests of reason in the physical sciences and technology have obviously and powerfully generated economic progress ever since the Industrial Revolution.

At the same time, individual lives and society have been subjected to rational innovation. The early bourgeoisie invented new standards of conduct: rational remunerative habits such as industriousness, thrift, and hygiene. They budgeted their lives—closely calculating their profits, risks, and satisfactions, and repressing temporary impulses for long-term goals.

Social theorists, beginning with Hobbes, began to study society scientifically too, convinced that human institutions, just like the steam engine, might be improved by intelligent inventors. That line of thought exploded into politics in the American and French Revolutions. Less exciting, but just as effectual, was the gradual rationalization of economic life through such changes as the increasing division of labor and the rising importance of efficiency and clock-measured time.

If poor people in developing countries are to overcome their poverty, they too must fully appropriate the power of reason. They must learn to order their personal lives more rationally—through family planning, to take a controversial example. Poor people in poor countries tend to have big families, partly so that a few children are likely to survive to care for the parents in their old age, but partly, too, for less rational motives: because family planning is a new-fangled idea, or because traditional religion forbids it.

Then, too, poor people must gain the revolutionary insight that oppressive social structures can be rationally criticized, debated, and reordered. Political pressure for social reform depends on literacy and popular rationality.

The remaining three of the six values I have taken to be representative of economic culture—*liberty, equality,* and *fraternity*—have been even more controversial than the ideals of *this-worldliness, progress,* and *rationality.* Virtually all modern societies confess their dedication to this-worldly progress through science and technology, but the world is divided between the political Right and Left in its interpretation of the social ideals of liberty, equality, and fraternity. These three ideals, once only spiritual insights, first became a world-reforming, pragmatic slogan through their association with the rising European bourgeoisie in the eighteenth and nineteenth centuries. The bourgeoisie interpreted liberty, equality, and fraternity in ways that were consistent with capitalism. But the proletariat, peasants, and colonies later seized on the same ideals, often interpreting them more radically in order to use them as weapons against the European bourgeoisie.

Liberty. The *liberty* which capitalism brought was only a boon to the bourgeoisie at first. Capitalism "tore asunder the motley feudal ties that bound man to his 'natural superiors,'" as Marx and Engels put it, but for the working class that meant leaving the security of traditional agriculture to work for uncertain wages in crowded and unsanitary cities.[14] Parliaments were increasingly powerful, but only property owners could vote. Free markets and free trade served primarily the bourgeoisie. The bourgeoisie were also the first to internalize liberty; they were uniquely individualistic and independent.

Gradually more and more people in the industrialized countries have come to enjoy liberty. Most of us now take it for granted that a young person can choose a career, rather than repeat what his parents have done. People are allowed to say and write almost whatever they think; dissent is allowed. In the United States, schools are expected to teach children to think for themselves. The best modern management techniques permit individuals to develop their own interests and potential, managers realizing that self-directed people with a sense of participation in decisions tend to be more creative and productive.

Poor, illiterate people in developing countries are not nearly so free. They are bound by sheer poverty and oppressed by their "superiors." Many are subjectively in bondage, too—submissive and fatalistic. That is why the educational theory of Paulo Friere is so powerful.[15] Friere argues that teaching the poor to read and write should be more than teaching them to memorize syllables or read what others have written. Literacy instruction should help the oppressed to "pronounce their own word"—to form their own concepts of the world, instead of remaining captive in the worldview their oppressors have taught them. When Friere's method was used in northeast Brazil, such subjective freedom led new literates into political action. The military government which came to power in 1964 jailed Friere and then suggested he leave the country. The "bottom-up" development that Friere's "cultural action for freedom" inspired was not the sort of development Brazil's ruling generals had in mind.

Equality. The capitalist interpretation of *equality* is equal opportunity. Extreme inequalities remain, but, ideally, everyone is at least given civil rights and a chance to compete for wealth and fame. Before capitalism, much less social mobility had been allowed. Today equal opportunity—that is, status by merit—underlies the system of rewards used throughout the developed world, including the richer Communist countries. Have so many societies changed simply because justice requires at least equal opportunity? No, they have changed partly because equal opportunity is conducive to economic growth.

Economic theory demonstrates what history had already shown: the economic efficiency of systems which issue rewards according to achievement. Discrimination by race or sex in a society blocks economic growth. If blacks or women are admitted to jobs from which they were previously barred, their gains in income do not come out of the paychecks of white males. The economy grows. The new workers earn their own keep. Capitalists stand to profit from the increased supply of labor, too. Wages for previously protected jobs will probably fall somewhat, but blacks and women will gain much more than white males lose.[16] Eventually, the general expansion of the economy may mean more demand for all goods and services, thus perhaps higher incomes even for white males.

This seems to have been the result of the massive immigration into the United States in the nineteenth century. The new immigrants did not, as some feared, throw the native labor force out of work. On the contrary, immigration proved to be an engine of growth. Had Germans, Irish, Swedes, Jews, Italians, Mexicans, and Slavs been successfully kept out, growth would have been slower.

Equality of opportunity makes economic sense. But is equality of opportunity enough? Reformers of capitalism have pointed to the needs of people who are not able to fend for themselves in open competition—the elderly, people with limited natural abilities, or single mothers who need to stay home with young children. Are such people also to experience full equality? If so, it will be due to a notion of equality which goes beyond the logic of economic growth, and the mechanism must be something other than unfettered capitalism.

Fraternity. Critics of capitalism claim that *fraternity* has little practical meaning in capitalist society. Capitalism broke traditional social bonds, moved people to anonymous cities, and inspired a hard-hearted ethic of rugged individualism. Industrialization was often ruthless in its early stages, the working class slaving long hours under foul conditions for survival wages.

The rise of capitalism was also associated, however, with a new sense of wider fraternity. Feudalism gave way to nation states and to international trade and travel. Because of the unity already achieved under capitalism, by the nineteenth century revolutionaries could realistically appeal to the workers of the world to unite.

A growing sense of universal brotherhood also underlay the increased honesty which distinguished some of the bourgeoisie in business dealings with strangers. Max Weber, in *The Protestant Ethic and the Spirit of Capitalism*, challenged the assumption that modern capitalism was ushered in by a wave of unscrupulous greed.[17] Webster's thesis has been debated ever since he proposed it. Many of the industrialists, planters, and traders who flourished during capitalism's heyday were anything but saints. But Weber argued that many of the pioneers of capitalism brought religious devotion to their worldly occupations. They considered their businesses opportunities for practical service, eschewed quick but dishonest gains, and endured ascetic schedules of work and investment. It might be said they impregnated commerce and industry with a bit of Christian fraternity.

Since then a long series of preachers have been able to "sell" the Golden Rule as a means to economic success. A famous nineteenth-century preacher in the United States, Russell Conwell, made the point in a sermon called "Acres of Diamonds" which he delivered 6000 times (earning millions of dollars for himself in the process).[18] In our century Norman Vincent Peale and Dale Carnegie taught a generation that faith and morality can be good business.[19] To some extent, the work ethic is now sustained by habit and greed, and the wheels of business are greased by superficial, self-serving friendliness. On the other hand, there are still many people who understand their work as a form of humanitarian service, and genuine dedication is still likely to result in high achievement.

All successful capitalist societies depend on some minimal sense of fraternity among the public in general. Capitalism does not function as well in societies where people tend to retain traditional, narrower loyalties—to tribe, family, or friends—at the expense of the public welfare. Relatively efficient systems of modern commerce (like checks and credit accounts) and of government (income tax and welfare programs) would not work at all unless most people could be trusted.

Simply working hard and not cheating each other much is a very limited form of fraternity, of course. Representatives of the working class and former colonial subjects have argued that real fraternity would mean sharing society's wealth. I will discuss this debate in Chapters 4 and 5.

In this introductory discussion I want to note that despite ideological differences, virtually all modern societies--both capitalist and socialist, both rich and poor—are at least theoretically committed to all three of these Enlightenment social values—*liberty, equality,* and *fraternity.* Critics of capitalism insist that it has failed to live up to these ideals, but they concur in the ideals which first entered practical politics with the rise of capitalism in Europe.

This-worldliness, progress, reason, liberty, equality, and *fraternity*—these six Enlightenment values represent the natural religion of the age. They are goals virtually everybody shares. Presidents appeal to them in speeches. Preachers refer to them at public baccalaureates, so that everyone can say amen. These values are the real religion of many people who consider themselves Christians, or Buddhists, or adherents of no religion at all. Even believers may sometimes have questions about doctrines like sacrificial atonement or the resurrection, but values like reason or liberty seem obvious and natural.

If Enlightenment values are somewhat misleading, we are—as individuals and as a society—profoundly misguided.

3

Twisted Affluence

There is a widespread sense in affluent countries like the United States that our life-styles and technologies are somehow askew—self-frustrating and, in some ways, immoral.

The original meaning for the words for sin in both Hebrew and Greek is "to miss the mark." Although *economic culture* has made the world much wealthier than ever before, modern affluence has somehow missed the mark. It does not satisfy. This "sin" is most obvious in the richest countries.

For the most part, however, popular misgivings about affluence have remained vague and ineffectual. They are not being focused into widespread personal and political reforms.

Perhaps a biblical perspective could help, both to identify the kinds of reforms which are necessary and to provide the motivation.

The moral ambiguity of modern prosperity can be diagnosed by understanding economic culture as a twisted reflection of God:

A reflection of God. . . . In this chapter the first three of the six values I have taken to be representative of economic culture will be seen to be rooted in and related to Christian ethics. This is because the ideals of modern culture grew out of the spiritual heritage of Europe, which was for centuries informed by Christian moral teaching. Although the economic culture which took shape with the Industrial Revolution and French Revolution is secular and sometimes antireligious, it is in many ways truer to Christian values than was the ostensibly Christian culture of the Middle Ages. This congeniality between Christianity and the modern world is not just my own idea, of course, but has been a major theme of liberal Christian theologians for much of the last two centuries.

. . . *but dangerously twisted.* In its popular, secularized form, economic culture is off target—sinful. It results in frustrating life-styles, and it makes people think that their own worth is based on how much they work or spend. Divorced from the worship of God, economic culture often becomes truncated, too. As I will explain further in Chapter 4, people tend to build their lives on some interpretation of this-worldly, rational progress, while neglecting whatever Enlightenment *social* values (liberty, equality, and fraternity) threaten their own interests.

To better understand what is wrong with modern materialism, it may help first to get a biblical view of what is right about it.[1] Otherwise, our criticism may be too sweeping, leading to vague guilt but to no specific reforms.

BIBLICAL ROOTS OF THIS-WORLDLINESS, PROGRESS, AND REASON

The modern values of this-worldliness, progress, and reason are all partly rooted in the Bible. The modern sense that this world is worthwhile, what I have called *this-worldliness*, harks back to the biblical creation story. God created the material world and called it "very good." Adam was to name the animals, giving meaning to creation, and to till the garden, maintaining it. He and Eve were to enjoy each other and eat every fruit but one.

According to the Bible, God continues to be involved in this world. Its well-being and development are important to him. His people are charged to obey him *in the world,* consecrating their ordinary functions in society and their particular moment in history.

Throughout the Bible this-worldly benefits—material prosperity, good reputation, health, long life, loving children, and security—are understood as blessings from God. When God blessed Abraham, Isaac, and Jacob, he promised them a rich land, as many children as there are stars in the sky, and such prosperity that all the nearby nations would benefit by being close to them. This-worldly blessings were considered good; poverty and adversity, bad. The Old Testament writers, however, also knew that wealth can lead to spiritual arrogance and hardheartedness toward the poor, so they gave some harsh warnings about this-worldly wealth.

The New Testament, even more than the Old, reminds us that those who are poor in the things of this world may be more open to God. The early Christians were somewhat detached from this-worldly concerns because of their eagerness for the Kingdom which Christ had promised. They expected his Second Coming at any moment.

Over the first few centuries of the Christian era this original tendency toward other-worldliness was accentuated by Hellenistic cultural influences such as Neoplatonism and Gnosticism, which taught disdain for the material world. When, centuries later, the Reformation reasserted the worthiness and importance of this world, it was, in part, because it had rediscovered the relative worldliness of the Bible. As Christians, we can be grateful for modern culture's sharp appetite for the good things of God's creation and its seriousness about this-worldly improvements.

The modern sense of *progress* is also rooted in the biblical experience. Ancient Israel, unlike the rest of the ancient world, believed that history was going somewhere new and better. The people of Israel learned to know the Lord when they were traveling through the desert. Their Lord was always on the move—freeing them from slavery, taking them to a new land, later punishing them with exile and promising a new creation, finally even taking on human flesh. He would never allow his people to become too settled.

In biblical history people make decisions which irrevocably change things. The people of Israel can choose not to obey God. In fact, the biblical writers characteristically view history as a drama of human sin and divine overcoming. Again and again, God's people fail to do their part. The patriarchs are undependable. Israel is idolatrous and hardhearted toward the poor. God's messengers are rejected; the Lord Incarnate is killed.

God judges sin, but more often he waits. Even prophets of doom had glorious visions of the future, because they knew that God could not bear to give people their due. The prophets looked forward to a new age when God's people would know and spontaneously obey him, when the Messiah would teach all nations. It would be an age of peace and prosperity. The deserts would bloom. The mountains would drip sweet wine. Everyday life would be consecrated; ordinary buckets and horsebells in the new Jerusalem would be inscribed, "Holy to the Lord" (Zech. 14:20).

Many of the early Christians expected these grand promises to be fulfilled during their lives. As time passed, however, it became evident that the Kingdom might be long delayed. Christians began to redirect their hopes, more toward individual life after death and less toward the promised transformation of the whole world.

For centuries relatively little progress was made in Christendom. Christian bishops established some pioneer institutions of mercy (hospitals, hotels, and feeding programs for the poor) in the late Roman Empire, and, during the chaotic centuries that followed, Christian monasteries were often enclaves of learning and advanced farming techniques. Many Christians during the Middle Ages certainly worked to protect and improve their societies out of a sense of devotion to God.

The rapid movement of modern progress began, however, about the time of pre-Reformation scholars like Thomas More and Erasmus, who called Christendom to reform itself. In fact, Europe did somewhat reform itself, and several centuries of steady progress gradually built up a belief in progress.

The antecedents of modern *reason* are more Greek and Roman than Hebrew. The Enlightenment tradition of scientific thinking is conscious of these classical origins and suspicious of faith. In the centuries leading up to the Enlightenment the Church discredited itself by opposing the rise of science, most dramatically in the censure of Galileo. Modern science was eventually welcomed as enthusiastically as it was, because it offered relief from the bloody, endless theological disputes which followed the Reformation.

The conflict between the rising ideal of rationality and Christianity need not have been as bitter as it was. Scientific thinking had its origins in Greece, but when Hellenistic Jews and Christians studied classical culture, many of them found the Greek conception of a Prime Mover who had infused matter with rationality to be consistent with what the Scriptures taught about God. The Jewish philosopher, Philo, wrote that God had created the world through his

logos, a Greek philosophic term meaning *divine reason.*
The Gospel of John calls Jesus Christ the *logos.*

The Scriptures had concentrated on God's laws for people, but from the very beginning (the creation hymn of
Genesis 1) they also praised God for the order in nature.
Just as the Lord had prescribed a law for mankind, the
Scriptures perceived that other creatures—night and day,
the sun and stars, water and land, living things—were also
governed by law.

Biblical faith made a more original contribution to modern rationality by exorcising the various gods and spirits
which once dominated people's lives. In this way, faith
cleared the way for a rational approach to problems. The
worship of idols, against which the prophets railed, had
substituted mumbo jumbo and arbitrary regulations for the
Lord's insistence on justice and mercy. Historically, the
spread of Christianity exorcised the dark powers which
had held much of the gentile world in their sway. Liberation from the "principalities and powers" was a major theme
in St. Paul's teaching: God, in His grace, became one of us,
not a demigod, so we need not fear any dark spirits or obey
their arbitrary laws.

One of the most exciting documents from the first centuries of the church is St. Athanasius' "Life of Anthony." It
tells how St. Anthony, the first hermit monk, defied the
fears of his contemporaries. It was thought that demons
haunted tombs and the desert, so that was precisely where
Anthony went to live. People flocked to this hero of faith
for healing and exorcism, and his example was followed
throughout the Roman Empire by thousands of other men
who became monks.[2]

The struggle against spiritual darkness continued during
the Middle Ages, as monks converted Europe and gradually
instructed Europeans in the faith. Browsing through library
stacks, I once happened upon a musty copy of a book by

Albertus Magnus, one of Thomas Aquinas' teachers. It explained the potions and prescriptions of magicians, with the express intention that the devil, the father of lies, could not then so easily exploit popular ignorance for evil purposes.

Scholastic theologians, best represented by Aquinas himself, were confident that all knowledge was godly. The Almighty Creator had revealed himself in Jesus. He is benevolent. Thus, mysterious forces in nature need not be held in awe; they can be investigated. God intends malevolent forces to be subjected to man in the end. Such faith, taken for granted, was a condition for the rise of science in the sixteenth century and the emergence of more rational, less superstitious patterns of personal behavior.

THE MORAL PATTERN OF BIBLICAL ECONOMICS

Despite such biblical roots, modern economic culture is obviously not godly. From a biblical point of view, what is wrong?

Much of the Old Testament is an inquiry into the wealth of nations. Economic teaching is especially prominent in Deuteronomy, the history books which follow it (Joshua, Judges, Samuel, Kings), and the prophets. But the biblical writers did not point, as I have done, to causal relations between cultural values and economic growth. They believed that the Lord was the only source of prosperity, and they taught, almost naively, that the way to continued prosperity was to love him and seek justice. They feared conquest and famine, the scourges of the ancient world, less than idolatry and hardheartedness toward the poor.

The prophets taught that history "swings on a moral hinge." [3] The moral pattern they perceived in the rise and fall of nations might be illustrated by the circle below:

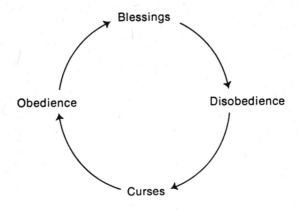

The pattern is as follows: God had promised to bless people with spiritual and material prosperity if they were faithful and righteous. Prosperity can be tempting, however. Rich people tend to focus on riches, forgetting God and the poor. The results, claim the Scriptures, are normally conflict and curses. It is only when people are at their wits' end that they are likely to fear God and reform. God rewards their obedience, and the cycle begins again.[4]

This cycle was demonstrated by Israel's history. The nation of Israel in slavery cried out to God; he was merciful and freed them. When they became secure and comfortable, however, they attributed the wealth to their own efforts. They devoted themselves to fertility itself, worshiping baals (nature gods) which promised riches without making the moral demands the Lord had made. Indifference toward the poor followed logically from amoral idolatry. Eventually, Israel suffered military conquest, as the prophets had threatened. The Old Testament historians and prophets attributed the downfall to unfaithfulness, particularly on the part of their kings. The immediate reason for the nation's fall was, in fact, that the monarchy had become unstable, and that was, in turn, because King David's successors were oppressive and immoral. Immorality in high places led slowly but inevitably—through civil strife, palace coups, and counter-coups—to the nation's destruction.

God's moral judgment is similarly evident in the lives of individuals, a theme which was developed in the Wisdom literature of the Old Testament. The Proverbs, for example, present two pictures of what a person's life can be:

The wicked fool is greedy for money and will cut corners in business to get it. The Proverbs admit he may get rich quickly, but they argue that eventually he is likely to get into trouble because of his dishonesty. In any case, he will be the sort of man who is likely to spend whatever money he has faster than he can make it.

The righteous man doesn't work all the time; he remembers the sabbath, but has worked for whatever wealth he has. Money is not the most important thing in his life, but he is prudent, no spendthrift, so he can always afford to be generous. Because creation is bountiful, he can almost be sure that an honest day's work will produce enough for his family—more than enough, something extra to give to the widow, the orphan, and the poor.

Life is not always so simple, of course. The Old Testament (especially Habakkuk, Job, and some of the Psalms) includes complaints that the righteous often suffer. Even more often, however, the Lord is patient with the wicked, so that immorality goes unpunished.

The New Testament is centered in God's patience with sinners. In the forgiving death and resurrection of Jesus Christ, God's grace short-circuited the moral pattern which the prophets had perceived, providing continued blessing despite human disobedience:

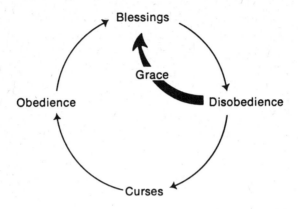

The New Testament sometimes echoes Old Testament optimism that God will bless the righteous. We are counselled to trust the Father to provide us with all we need. Paul's injunctions to work and be charitable retrace the Proverbs' picture of the man blessed in this world—working, trusting, moderate, and generous. This is still God's earth, so that common morality is often rewarded by success.

But this is also a world in rebellion against God. The New Testament writers witnessed the Righteous Man crucified. Because God's justice gave way to mercy in Christ Jesus, the New Testament is less confident of worldly rewards and punishments, more aware that it is often the most loving people who bear the brunt of human wickedness. Jesus urges us beyond common morality. "Leave everything and follow me," he said.

Jesus represents a radical break from the status quo, also in economic terms. He was born among the poor—a humble young woman, shepherds at work, a carpenter. His ministry was mainly among outcasts (women, gentiles, tax collectors, and public sinners), and after his resurrection it was mainly lower-class gentiles who accepted the gospel of sin and grace.

Two New Testament writers, Luke and James, virtually equate wealth with wickedness; the rest of the New Testament makes a more careful distinction between wealth itself and the sins characteristically associated with it—arrogance, greed, and injustice. All the New Testament writers agree, however, that it is exceptionally difficult for any rich person to be saved.

IDOLATROUS MATERIALISM

Since both the Old and New Testaments link economics to right worship and morality (the New Testament only more emphatic about the dangers of wealth and more demanding in its call to faith and sharing), we might consider whether the anomalies of modern affluence are due to idolatry and injustice. Could it be that the values of modern culture, although rooted in the revelation of God, have been distorted by idolatry, with idoltary lending itself to injustice? If so, how would our behavior change if we continued to hold these values, but combined them with devotion to God and service to other people?

The this-worldliness typical of our times is clearly idolatrous and immoral, based in insecure and self-centered cravings. By contrast, the "simple living movement" in the United States today illustrates what *Christian this-worldliness* might be. The "simple living movement" had its origins in the counterculture among young people in the 1960s, but most of the people involved in it are older and in families. Their decisions for alternative ways of living are more deliberate and more likely to be lasting. Much of the movement is within the churches, drawing inspiration from biblical teaching concerning wealth.

I have been impressed with the efforts one of my sisters and her family have been making to live more simply. They have made a studied attempt to adjust their home economics to their understanding of God's intentions and world problems. They are trying to extricate themselves from the hectic, highly processed style of family life which is now prevalent. They have changed their diet, buying patterns, and daily routines. They joined one of the Alternatives Celebrations study-action groups springing up in congregations across the country, beginning to reorder their lives by devising less commercial, more meaningful ways to celebrate holidays. They are spending more time with their children and each other, less with television. They have tried to free themselves from images of store-bought success that advertisements and commercial culture peddle. They give generously to some selected charities, and they are deeply engaged in political issues.[5]

The simple living movement has given rise to several helpful organizations:

• The one in which my sister is involved is called *Alternatives* (1924 East Third Street, Bloomington, Indiana 47401). It began in 1973 with the publication of Bob Kochtitzky's *Alternative Christmas Catalogue*. Most people, including non-Christians, find the commercialization of Christmas in the United States inappropriate. The *Catalogue* described ways of celebrating Christmas that would be oriented less toward consumption, more toward national and international justice. We express our values and priorities in our celebrations, so Kochtitzky thought people might begin to reform their lives if they could at least make the celebration of Christmas more consistent with the Spirit of Jesus. His annual publication, later expanded to include other celebrations too, is now called the *Alternative Celebrations Catalogue*. At the end of 1977 the National Alternative Celebrations Campaign was launched, with the goal of organizing 1000 study-action groups throughout the United States.

• Another simple-living organization is called the *Shakertown Pledge Group* (c/o Friends Meeting, West 44th and York South, Minneapolis, MN 55410). It began at a national meeting of religious retreat center directors in Shakertown, Kentucky, in 1973. Having reflected on the global problems of poverty and resource scarcity, some of them decided to commit themselves to lives of "creative simplicity." They drafted and signed what came to be known as the Shakertown Pledge, and began to campaign nationally to have others join them in the Pledge. They publish a newsletter called *Creative Simplicity*.

• A third organization worth mentioning is called *Sojourners*, a theologically conservative, but politically radical religious community (1309 L Street, N.W., Washington, DC 22005). They publish a magazine called *Sojourners*, which deals with the quest for modest, committed styles of life, as well as national and international justice. Its circulation has increased spectacularly over the last five years. What has made it so attractive? Partly, it interests people because its authors personally evidence their commitments by sharing all their goods in common and by reduced levels of consumption.

The simple living movement is not other-worldly. It is directed toward life-styles which are more satisfying and toward this-worldly reform. In the words of the Shakertown Pledge:

> We intend to reduce the frills and luxuries of our present life-style but at the same time to emphasize the beauty and joy of living. We do this for three reasons: first, so that our own lives can be more simple and gracious, freed from attachment to material goods; second, so that we are able to release more of

our wealth to share with those who need the basic
necessities of life; third, so that we can move toward
a Just World Standard of Living in which each person
shares equally in the earth's resources.[6]

All this is perhaps less simple and more organized than
it need be. It occurs to me that Latin cultures, for example
have inherited a gift for simple, hearty living, while North
Americans habitually organize and propagandize, even
when the goal is simplicity.

Nevertheless, those who have been touched by the movement testify that they are spending less and enjoying it
more. They say their lives are more satisfying—more focused, freer, open to God and simple pleasures. They echo
Gandhi, who wrote that "the deliberate and voluntary re-
duction of wants" would not only increase capacity for service, but also yield real happiness.[7]

How can this be? It is possible to increase satisfaction by
decreasing money income and consumption, because, as
Alan Watts, a Buddhist philosopher, suggested, slavish
materialism is not really this-worldly at all:

> Our radically misnamed "materialistic" civilization
> must above all cultivate the love of material, of earth,
> air, water, of mountains and forests, of excellent food
> and imaginative housing and clothing, and of cherish-
> ing and artfully erotic contact between human
> bodies.[8]

People work for money, an abstraction, without taking
time to savor the good things money can buy. We rush
through the present moment to "save time," another abstraction, and thus suffer chronic disappointment. Why?
Because our egos crave the reassurance of having more
money and getting more accomplished.

Watts recommends the Buddhist solution: to realize that
one's own ego is an illusion. Even better, I suggest, is the

possibility of being liberated from self-debasing idolatries by divine grace: the ego forgiven and justified by God.

If we allow our fundamental sense of self-worth to depend on things—what we earn or spend, what we do or have—rather than resting on God's approval of us, we become vulnerable to mammon's terrible judgments. Middle-aged men may become frustrated with life because they have not made enough of themselves. Homemakers may feel almost ashamed because they do not earn money for their work. Or children may be embarrassed because their families cannot afford all the good things their friends have. There is never enough of anything in this finite world for us to prove ourselves in these fetishistic ways. We can always work more, do better, own better. We are always inadequate.

Grace can free us from the need to justify ourselves with the things of this world, so that we can relax and enjoy them. God's grace has a dimension which is out of this world, but encourages—like nothing in the world—a hearty and holy materialism.

The sort of faith in progress which is typical of the modern world is also idolatrous. It expects too much from ourselves and too little from God. The alternative is *Christian hope*.

The over-ambitiousness of secular belief in progress is exemplified by some of the anomalies of modern health care. A good reference on this issue is *Medical Nemesis* (New York: Pantheon, 1976) by Ivan Illich, perhaps the best example of a social critic with Christian doubts about "progress." [9] Health is really more a matter of personal habits than sophisticated treatment, and suffering requires grace even more than it requires the latest equipment. Many, if not most, hospital cases are complicated by moral and spiritual problems like drinking, smoking, careless diet, violence, psychosomatic disorders, or spiritual malaise. Yet medical treatment is administered as if health depended primarily on the progress of medical technology.

"Progress" has even been extended to the burial business: steel caskets, vaults, and air-conditioned mausoleums. Fortunately, there are now organizations in many cities that help people plan simple funerals for themselves—to save money and, more important, to be honest about decay.

A friend of mine is a chaplain in a state mental asylum. I say "asylum," not hospital, because my friend has taught me the limitations of the "medical progress" analogy in dealing with disturbed people. In fact, virtually none of the people in this particular facility is likely ever to be cured. They are generally low-income, friendless people who have not been able to cope with the normal demands of society for many years. They can be counseled or helped with medications, but they are not likely to change much. My friend, after several years as a chaplain among them, has concluded that the hospital administration confuses the issue when they ask staff to go through elaborate goal-setting exercises for each patient, or rate staff according to the number of dismissals, and appeal to the state legislature for funds as a "hospital." Better care could be provided if there were not unrealistic pressure for "progress."

I am not suggesting that society should give less care to these patients. For the Christian at least, recognizing that we are virtually helpless in confronting a certain evil is no reason to give up hope.

Hope in humanly impossible situations was dramatized for me when my wife and I visited a hospital which Mother Teresa's order of nuns operates for indigent people in Calcutta. We went through ward after ward of near hopelessness. My wife and I were most impressed by an Indian woman, Sister Barbara, who showed us around the hospital. Sister Barbara was one of the few nuns who started with Mother Teresa a generation ago, providing beds and a bit of dignity to indigents dying on the streets outside a Hindu temple of death.

As Sister Barbara took us through the men's tubercular ward that day, an old man, shrivelled and thin, groaned and nearly rolled off his cot; she lifted his leg back onto the cot and covered him again with his shirt. As she showed us the ward for sick orphans, she must have held or touched a dozen children—each afraid, lonely, and ill. We were depressed by the massive and severe suffering in that place, but Sister Barbara went about her work with radiant joy.

It was hope like hers—undaunted by misery, danger, or death—that led from Mother Teresa's original household of nuns to the establishment of the worldwide network of services for the poor which Mother Teresa's order now administers. Sister Barbara's hope is not based on the order's successes, however, but on what God may do—in history and beyond it.

The extravagance of biblical promises inspires Christian action in the face of the most intractable evils. In comparison to the prophetic hopes for God's Kingdom, the most optimistic goals of modern progress seem modest. Secular faith in progress seldom dares look for more than a gradual alleviation of poverty and ignorance, while the Bible teaches us to hope for the end of all suffering, sin, and alienation. It promises more than we can imagine—the reversal of decay and the resurrection of the dead. Such radical hopes can inspire, as Latin America's liberation theologians have discovered, creative social action and new visions of what society might be.[10]

Just as God's grace, which transcends the world, can help us to relax and enjoy the things of this world, his extravagant promises for the future allow us to be more realistic about the present and irrepressible in working for progress.

Finally, although faith stretches beyond reason, *faith can help us to be rational.* Modern "rationality" is too often characterized by sophisticated means toward ultimately nonsensical ends. We may have, for the most part, escaped from astrology, spooks, and magic, but have instead fallen subject to various modern forms of fetishism and idolatry.

As individuals, we overwork and overconsume. Most people in affluent countries seem to be squandering their affluence in bizarre and unsatisfying ways. Many are like the mad child in D. H. Lawrence's story, "The Rocking Horse Winner." He constantly heard voices in his family's house, saying, "There must be more money! There must be more money!" The child raced himself to death on a rocking horse, just as we drive ourselves—never satisfied, never catching up with our desires. We are lured on by advertisements, the hundreds we see each day. We are subtly pressured by the people we love, who are also tempted to measure their worth by what they buy.

Some people—myself included—are less tempted by consumer goods than by the satisfactions of prestige, power, or work itself. Thousands of intelligent individuals who carefully plan their lives, perhaps even preparing daily lists of things to do, somehow let those lists of minor tasks take control, so that they seldom find time for some of the things they consider most important—children, for example, or prayer.

At the social level, too, we sometimes fail to be rational. Our two most pressing national problems are "stagflation" and limited resources. But in each case, much of the public seems reluctant to be resolute in dealing with the problem.

Inflation has become so ingrained over the last decades, accelerating in the 1970s, that even high unemployment has not lowered it to tolerable levels. Inflation makes money less useful to people, because it no longer holds its value. Unpredictable inflation introduces uncertainty into all sorts of planning, contracts, and investment decisions.

Yet more serious, say economists, may be the long-term moral effects of chronic, accelerating inflation:

> Inflation has capricious effects on the income and wealth of a nation's families, and this inevitably causes disillusionment and discontent. Social and political frictions tend to multiply, and the very foundations of a society may be endangered.
>
> —*Arthur Burns,*
> *Former Chairman, Federal Reserve Board* [11]

> Inflation is like a country where nobody speaks the truth.
>
> —*Henry Wallich,*
> *Federal Reserve Board* [12]

> It is not only the change of a mechanical system that is worrisome. If the currency bloats, what does it do to the people? Do high school students change their outlooks? If paper money makes fools of savers and rewards the speculator instead of the workers, what replaces those Protestant ethic bastions of work and saving? —*Adam Smith* [13]

In the terms of this book, unpredictable inflation mocks rationality and dedication to progress in personal planning. Since it gives some kinds of people—politicians and government employees, unionized workers, the young, and perhaps debtors—unearned gains at the expense of other groups in society, it tends to erode the underlying sense of fairness and fraternity which free societies need to maintain political stability.

What must be done to bring inflation down? The experts have various suggestions, but nearly all agree that governments, including the U.S. government, will have to maintain firm and steady policies, tolerating a certain amount of inflation and a certain amount of unemployment, in order to steer the course back to stable prices and economic expansion. There are no quick and easy solutions.

Can U.S. voters avoid the temptation to apparently quick and easy solutions? We have enjoyed the longest sustained period of economic growth in history. People's personalities and sense of self-worth have come to depend on continued growth. Growth is almost a god. Voters are tempted to pressure politicians to lower taxes and increase spending. Such measures have given us spurts of higher consumption, but only at the cost of higher and higher inflation. Some pollsters tell us people in the United States are more unanimously concerned about inflation than any issue since the Second World War, but can we muster the self-restraint to overcome it? [14]

Popular reluctance to come to terms with resource scarcity is even more obvious. We cannot continue present patterns of consuming mineral resources indefinitely. A number of ecologically disastrous technologies (nuclear weapons, high-powered automobiles, nonbiodegradable and poisonous chemical products) must be brought under control. Some people—notably E. F. Schumacher, author of *Small Is Beautiful*—have suggested that the gigantic scale of modern technologies destroys human and social resources too, by requiring huge organizations, decreasing the scope of democratic decision-making, and introducing unpredictable changes on a dangerously massive scale.[15]

We need to examine each of these resource problems in detail, weigh alternatives, and adjust. Yet many people resist—as if cheap gas were a sacred totem, carelessness about the environment an inalienable right, or awesome technologies an almost religious fascination.

It would be incorrect to attribute all these irrationalities in private and public life to the modern divorce of rationality from God. Some of these problems which seem obvious now were not at all apparent a few years ago, and it takes time to change. At the personal level, we are still adjusting to the higher levels of affluence gained over the last generation. Some of the more garish anomalies in the normal U.S. life-style of the 1950s and 1960s—rocket-like fins, a penchant for getting everything new, the single-minded drive for higher money incomes—are being corrected as people finally learn how to enjoy the higher incomes gained during those decades. Similarly, it takes time to notice and react to social problems. It took some time, for example, to recognize that inflation was no longer a temporary phenomenon or to notice the ecological crisis. It will require more time to find and implement solutions.

The malaise is deeper, however. Some of the irrationalities in typical American life-styles have been diagnosed for decades. The energy "crisis" was already obvious in 1974.

There is an underlying problem of idolatry. Ancient Israel was tempted to worship the proximate causes of their prosperity—agricultural fertility, the sun and rain, numerous children. Similarly, the immediate sources of prosperity in modern society—possessions, professional success, boom times, abundant resources, or whatever—can become fetishes. The temptation is to place our faith and hope in these proximate causes, forgetting the ultimate Giver. That is how we end up using sophisticated means to nonsensical ends.

When we make gods of limited and amoral things, human life—our lives—become debased and somewhat foolish:

> Their land is filled with idols;
> > they bow down to the work of their hands,
> > to what their own fingers have made.
> So man is humbled . . . (Isa. 2:8-9).

Divine grace can release us from materialistic fetishes—like money or constant growth—and give us the inner security we need to examine our lives and society with equanimity. Faith in God provides a moral direction to our lives, putting technology and personal cleverness within the rational context of moral order.

Just as a spiritual dimension to life lets us enjoy material things more fully, and hope in the Lord helps us to be more genuinely progressive, faith encourages rationality.

In summary, the first three modern values—this-worldliness, progress, and reason—are partially rooted in biblical experience, but only partially. Christian this-worldliness should be hearty in enjoyment, but, unlike secular this-worldliness, modest in accumulation. A Christian who is working toward progress will be hopeful and persistent, but relatively pessimistic about human achievement. Finally, although faith is not a reasoned conclusion, faith in Jesus Christ should encourage Christians to live and think sensibly.

The next chapter deals with the other three of the six values which constitute economic culture—liberty, equality, and fraternity. They, too, are each rooted in God's character, but they have been separated and set against one another in the class conflict and ideological division of the modern world.

4

Integrity in a
Broken World

The entire modern world is involved in one overarching political debate—the debate between capitalism and individualism on one hand, socialism and sharing on the other.

In extreme form, this issue separates the world into two blocs, Communist and capitalist. The 15,000-mile border between the two hostile ideologies, stretching from Finland to Korea, is still relatively closed and bristles with arms.

In more moderate form, the same issue separates exceptionally capitalistic countries like the United States or Switzerland from countries like Britain, West Germany, and Sweden, which have more fully developed social welfare programs.

People in the United States often look at Britain to see how social welfare programs might function in the United States, because the two countries share much of the same cultural and political heritage. More often than not, Americans think first about British economic problems, generally associating slow growth and balance of payments problems with bloated social welfare programs. But the British people I know recognize other factors which have contributed to their country's relative economic decline, and, in any case, they are not much attracted by the fierce individualism and hard-edged capitalism of the United States. Some wish British tax laws did not discourage private initiative as much as they do, but few would be willing to give up national health insurance and return to a system like ours under which low-income people often receive inadequate medical care. Some see a direct connection—as I do—between the lack of social welfare support and the high rate of violent crime in the United States.

Just as different countries within the capitalist West range along a spectrum from Right to Left, different Communist countries are more or less tolerant of individual freedom and initiative. Relatively liberal countries like Yugoslavia and Rumania are closer to Britain and West Germany on the political spectrum than are hard-line, more state-dominated countries like the U.S.S.R. and East Germany.

The debate between capitalism and socialism is particularly heated in many developing countries. In some countries the debate has inspired both dictatorships and terrorism, and in some, like Vietnam, Zimbabwe, and Nicaragua, armed conflict.

Every country has its local issues which have nothing to do with economic organization, but isn't it remarkable that there is *one* political debate in which virtually the entire world is engaged?

Within countries different political parties agitate for movement in one direction or the other. The same basic issue between Right and Left resurfaces again and again in debates over many specific questions like social health insurance, government regulation of the oil companies, or local taxes and school expenditures.

Individuals take their own positions within this worldwide debate, most obviously by the way they vote, but also by their life-styles. Some of the practical differences at the individual level are illustrated by the lives of two particular couples I know:

• George and Susan, about thirty years old, have just purchased a new, suburban home. A big chunk of their income goes for house payments, and much of their time is spent in decorating the house. Both come from modest middle-class backgrounds. George, with a degree in business, is rising rapidly in the management of a fast-foods chain. Susan works for an insurance company. Both are political conservatives, especially George, who loves to make jokes about government inefficiencies. They are members of their neighborhood Baptist church, attend every Sunday, and sponsor their church's youth group. They are loyal and generous friends.

• Dave is my pastor. He and his wife, Lois, are about fifty years old. They serve a Lutheran church in a low-income neighborhood of downtown Washington, he as pastor and she as a counsellor for people in need who are served by the congregation's social outreach programs. The congregation is small, and their salaries are modest. Although they are nearly twice George and Susan's age, they drive an older car and their home is more modest than the one George and Susan have bought. They are political liberals. Dave's sermons regularly remind us of the need for both personal and political action against social evils like racism and poverty.

A person's political position shapes not only his political views and votes, but also influences where he lives, what he buys, and the sort of job he chooses to do.

It can be tedious to discuss the basic differences which cause people to opt for the Left or Right in politics. We have heard many of the arguments before. If broader political questions like inter-country differences in economic organization are raised, people may become disinterested. If the discussion gets closer to home, most people already have strong opinions.

It may, however, be possible to learn something new about the schism between capitalist and socialist tendencies in modern politics and culture by reviewing it in the context of basic religious values. The split between Left and Right is obviously an economic issue, but it also has a religious dimension. Even small shifts in our attitudes toward this well-worn issue would produce significant practical changes.

THE SPLIT BETWEEN LEFT AND RIGHT

Capitalism emerged in Europe as modern economic development began. The relatively static medieval economy of traditional rights and prices gave way to entrepreneurship and change. A series of British thinkers—Adam Smith, Bentham, Ricardo, Malthus, and John Stuart Mill—explained what was happening and provided capitalism's theoretical justification.[1]

The publication of the *Communist Manifesto* in 1847 might be considered the birth of modern socialism. By the beginning of the First World War socialism had become a powerful mass movement, and class revolution was possible in several countries. In 1917 Lenin's Bolsheviks took control of the Russian empire.[2]

Both capitalism and socialism have changed considerably since the first decades of conflict between them. The standard of living for workers in Europe and North America has risen dramatically, and capitalism is now normally supported by a large government-controlled, planned sector. In all the developed "capitalist" countries government accounts for 15-25% of consumption and about 15% of capital formation (35% including public corporations).[3] The major socialist parties in Western Europe and North America are moderate, well-established and committed to parliamentary change. The West is more "capitalist" than the Communist states, but it is no longer, if it ever was, governed by *laissez faire*. Moreover, what survey data exist indicate that altruistic behavior is at least as frequent among individuals in capitalist societies as in any other.[4]

Marxist-Leninism has changed too. It is no longer just an opposition doctrine. Communism expanded quickly after the Second World War, through Russian conquest in Eastern Europe, and through the armed strength of Communist guerillas who had led opposition to Right-wing foreign occupation in China, North Korea, North Vietnam, and Yugoslavia. Now it is the establishment ideology for over a third of the world's population. The major business of Communism is no longer revolution, but routine economic management and planning. Political debate is not as open as in the West, but the debate between reformers (in favor of increased economic and civil liberties) and more Stalinist traditionalists mirrors political debate in the West.

At one level, the issue everywhere is between two forms of economic organization: markets versus bureaucracy. Other forms of social organization have not worked well to structure the bread-and-butter functions of a large and growing economy. Customary obligations and reciprocal sharing, for example, work well only in small groups like an African village or a religious congregation. A wave of inspiration can help make an economy work in wartime, but major attempts to generate peacetime growth with revolutionary zeal (the first years of the Russian Revolution, the Great Leap Forward and Cultural Revolution in China, and Cuba's attempts in the first years after its revolution to use "guerilla tactics" of economic management) were all, at least in the short run, economic failures.[5]

Thus, in considering ways of organizing modern economic affairs, we are usually left to choose between free markets (supply and demand) or bureaucratic planning. The simplest level of the debate between capitalism and socialism is whether markets or planning works best.

The paragraphs below represent aspects of the markets versus planning debate. Arguments for socialism (planning) and capitalism (markets) can be matched in opposing pairs. Those for socialism and against capitalism appear on the left, related arguments for capitalism and against socialism on the right:

SOCIALISM   CAPITALISM

1. What is produced?

Planning produces for need, not profit. To make money capitalists have to figure out how to satisfy people's desires in ways that will convince them to spend a lot of money. Thus, capitalism squanders precious resources. Even worse, it does not respond to the needs of the poor.

Should bureaucrats or people themselves decide what is needed? The products of socialist enterprises tend to be grim, colorless, and standardized. Consumer goods are often not available in Communist countries in the types and quantities consumers desire to buy.

2. How efficiently?

Capitalism might be economically efficient if the real world were characterized by numerous competitors in any field (what economists call "perfect competition"). In fact, modern capitalism is dominated by a few hundred huge corporations. Some markets, steel manufacturing

Many parts of modern capitalist economies do approximate the "perfect competition" of economic theory, and are thus remarkably efficient. Even oligopolistic industries are probably more efficient than the state-run monopolies in socialist countries. In competing with each for example, include just a few companies (what economists call "oligopoly"). Oligopolistic competition leads to higher prices and smaller quantities than would be efficient. The companies tend to compete only through advertising or by devising—or pretending they have devised —new and improved products.

other, oligopolies resort to deceptive and wasteful advertising, but their competition also results in a pleasing variety of goods.

3. How stable is the economy?

Capitalism still swings back and forth between boom times and recessions. A capitalist economy consists mainly of millions of people and corporations making decisions on the basis of their own self-interest. There is no mechanism which can keep the whole economy on a steady keel. "Keynesian" methods of macroeconomic control have not been able to avoid world recession, and have staved off depression only at the cost of inflation.

Combinations of administrative errors, moods, and movements also generate swings from good times to bad in socialist countries. In the capitalist countries modern macroeconomic management has succeeded in moderating business cycles. Depression has been avoided at the cost of only mild inflation. Currently high rates of inflation are due partly to the imprudent use of "Keynesian" controls by many governments. Better, steadier management should lead to prosperity and stable prices again.

4. Is economic growth encouraged?

The U.S.S.R.'s economic "take-off" in the 1930s under Stalin dramatized how rapidly a planned economy can grow. The economies of Eastern Europe continued to grow slightly faster than those of

Japan's "take-off" matched that of the U.S.S.R., and the richer capitalist countries have recently more than matched the growth pace of Eastern Europe. It is difficult to evaluate successes and

Western Europe until about 1960. China and North Korea also seem to have impressive growth records, and all the developing countries with Communist governments have made substantial progress toward meeting basic human needs.

failures in countries like China, North Korea, and Cuba, where governments control the flow of information. Some of the "economic miracles" among the developing countries (Taiwan, South Korea, Brazil) have been sparked by classic capitalist policies. Moderate socialist countries in Africa and Asia have tended to grow more slowly than more capitalist neighbors (Tanzania vs. Kenya, or Ghana vs. Ivory Coast; Burma and Indonesia vs. Thailand, Malaysia, and the Philippines; India and Sri Lanka vs. Pakistan).[6]

I have summarized here only points which have some validity. Even considering this relatively straightforward question—whether markets or bureaucratic planning more effectively delivers the goods—there are strong arguments on both sides.

TWO SPIRITUAL DIRECTIONS

More profoundly, the opposition between socialism and capitalism is a clash between fundamental modern values. This moral tension, not the more mundane markets versus planning debate, is what lends furor and idealism to the issue.

The slogan of the French Revolution, "Liberty, Equality, Fraternity," turns out to be an explosive combination. Capitalism fosters liberty, but often at the expense of equality and fraternity. Socialism may serve equality and fraternity, but has been less careful about individual liberties. It is the same divergence of values—between freedom on the one hand, equality and fraternity on the other—which leads the two couples I described above to choose different styles of life. George and Susan build a beautiful private life for themselves in the suburbs, while Dave and Lois forfeit private satisfactions for the sake of solidarity with the poor.

The political Left is, more obviously than the Right, a spiritual movement—an answer to the groanings of the oppressed. Demanding *equality* for oppressed classes and minorities has been a consistent theme of the Left. Equal opportunity is a first step, but giving everybody an equal chance does not satisfy the conscience of the Left if wide disparities still remain between rich and poor because of differences in abilities or historic injustices.

In the time of Marx and Lenin *compassion* for the proletariat gave way to the *organization* of the proletariat. Exploitation of the working class would not be ended by sermons or utopian schemes. Capitalism seemed to be simplifying the complexities of class into a simple, obnoxious dichotomy between bourgeoisie and proletariat; a classless, egalitarian society could be achieved, it was argued, by one final war between classes. There are places in the world today, too, where inequalities are similarly obnoxious, almost begging for revolution—South Africa and several countries in Latin America.

Some of the developing countries which have experienced rapid, capitalist growth have also suffered increasing inequality. The strong seized new opportunities, while the weak were left behind. "Development" became a sour word for many Latin American intellectuals during the Alliance for Progress years. The construction of factories, skyscrapers, and middle-class housing boomed, but peasant life changed little, and more and more of the poor flocked to barely habitable slums on the hills, ravines, and swamps of Latin American cities. In two important historic cases in

Asia and Africa—Pakistan and Nigeria—old ethnic conflicts were strained by increasing economic inequality to the point of civil war. Mahbub ul Haq, one of the architects of Pakistan's rapid growth in the 1960s, now frankly writes that he and his colleagues were wrong to pursue rapid capitalist growth so single-mindedly. He now recommends a more egalitarian style of development which is, in some ways, modeled after the People's Republic of China.[7]

Socialism is also inspired, as the word implies, by the aspiration for social wholeness—*fraternity*. Socialism's earliest advocates were appalled at the cruel individualism of the Industrial Revolution, nostalgic for times when the economy had been firmly embedded in human community. "Bourgeois economics" has focused on supply and demand, abandoning medieval notions of a "just price" that depends on need, custom, and other considerations we have come to regard as "non-economic." Socialists, however, insist that market relationships are only one strand within broader social relations. The market wage is not necessarily moral, even if hungry peasants are pouring in from the countryside eager to work on any terms.

Capitalism fosters competitive individualism, greed, and envy. De Tocqueville noticed this just after the French Revolution:

> Since money has not only become the sole criterion of a man's social status but has also acquired an extreme mobility—that is to say it changes hands incessantly, raising or lowering the prestige of individuals and families—everybody is feverishly intent on making money or, if already rich, on keeping his wealth intact.[8]

Capitalism may encourage freedom and creativity, but also confusion, conflict, purposelessness, and crime.

The fraternal spirit socialism claims to encourage may,

over the long run, become a powerful force for economic growth. In an interesting essay entitled "Raising Peanut Yields," published in Peking by the Foreign Language Press in 1972, an agricultural researcher named Yao-Shih-chang related how he overcame the temptation to neglect an experiment with peanut growth because of inclement weather:

> One rainy night I went out only after struggling with the thought that one night's absence wouldn't matter much. Then I remembered Chairman Mao's teaching . . . How could I learn the laws governing the growth of peanuts if I did not apply Chairman Mao's philosophic ideas, first of all, to think always of serving the proletariat? I got a good soaking that night and was chilled through, but . . . from that time on I persisted in making my observations rain or shine.[9]

Such socialist morality—sacrificial work and scrupulous honesty in service to the Chinese proletariat—is reminiscent of the worldly asceticism among early Calvinist businessmen which Max Weber described in *The Protestant Ethic and the Spirit of Capitalism.* It was inspired, however, not by religion, but by a heightened sense of national fraternity.

Capitalism's spiritual dimensions are less obvious than socialism's. In capitalism's defense, there is, first, a sense of innocence about modern wealth. Socialism's protests for justice and community echo biblical critiques of the rich, but the moral character of wealth has changed since Bible times. In ancient Israel, a simple agricultural society, the only means to accumulate wealth was military aggression: booty and tribute. Modern technology, however, produces riches which do not depend on rapacity. The close association of wealth with wickedness in Luke and James—or Marx and Lenin—is no longer always appropriate.[10]

Capitalism can also be defended from the natural-law tradition. When Adam Smith wrote about an "invisible hand" in the marketplace, he evoked this tradition of Christian philosophy which recognizes God's governance in the natural world. Instincts of self-preservation, as well as compassion, are God-given, and the world works tolerably well without special grace or exceptional morality.[11] Smith recognized that if each person pursues his own goals through trade, the mechanism of supply and demand makes resources available to those various goals with uncanny efficiency.

Studying the theory of trade, which has grown from Adam Smith's perspective, irrevocably complicated my own vision of the world. I went from seminary to graduate school in economics primarily because I was concerned about charges of U.S. imperialism. At that time my analysis of big corporations, for example, was primarily in terms of power. I was suspicious—as I still am—of such massive concentrations of power in relatively few hands. But in studying economics I learned the subtler logic of trade, and came to appreciate that even big corporations have to earn their keep, also in developing countries, by providing goods and services their clients cannot get as cheaply elsewhere.

A third ethical argument for capitalism is the most important: that capitalism has been somewhat more successful than socialism in protecting personal *liberty*. Socialists have tended to look to the state to help the poor and unite the nation, but the accumulation of power in the state also allows it to impose itself on people. Capitalism does not guarantee liberty, nor is socialism necessarily the road to slavery. Hundreds of dictatorships have presided over capitalist economies, and a number of countries have moved a long way toward socialism while retaining a high degree of freedom. Yet there does seem to be a historical and causal connection between capitalism and individual liberty.

Even relatively modest government measures to effect justice and care for needy citizens often do have costs in terms of regimentation and bureaucratic regulation. And the extreme Left has been flagrant in its abuses of individual liberty; virtually every Communist state has been a police state, where individual freedoms—to speak, travel, publish, worship—have been generally denied. Concentrations of power in capitalist countries (in corporations, for example) can also be oppressive, but at least they are opposed by countervailing concentrations of power (unions, for example), and they lack direct police power.[12]

Even in very poor countries where effective democracy is unlikely, capitalism can foster a spirit of freedom and creativity. I think, for example, of the wild variety of life-styles and products in market cities like Nairobi or Bangkok, in comparison to the relative uniformity of socialist cities like Havana, Rangoon, or even East Berlin. Capitalism in developing countries also leads to the formation of an independently minded middle-class, which is eventually likely to demand representative government and civil liberties.

HAVING IT BOTH WAYS

The division of economic culture into two opposing tendencies is due, in part, to inherent tensions between liberty, on the one hand, and equality and fraternity on the other. Those tensions are aggravated, however, by the opposing interests of different social classes. When it comes to practical politics, both the Right and Left rely more on self-interest than idealism. The Right represents the interests of people who are relatively well-off, while the Left mobilizes the poorer classes to get a bigger share of society's wealth. The different ways in which the Right and Left translate moral values into policy are generally consistent with the opposing interests of their two constituencies. We tend to support politicians who argue with moral conviction for policies that will benefit us.

Liberty, equality, and fraternity are *all three* found in the biblical revelation of God, but the combination of all three leaves little to self-interest. Christians experience freedom and love as *one dynamic*, not as opposing tendencies.

Freedom and love were already joined in the ethos of the Old Testament. The Old Testament law, given to a people just freed from slavery, breathes a respect for the liberty and equality of each person. It also urges practical fraternity. The law commanded, for example, that one should not even glean one's own field completely, but should leave food behind for the widow, the orphan, and the needy. There was a limit to what creditors could take if a debtor defaulted, and every seventh year was to be a sabbath year at which time things reverted to their original owners (Deuteronomy 15), giving everyone a fresh start and keeping extremes of wealth and power from developing. Greek and Roman politicians paid their dues of bread and circuses to the plebs, but our sense that individual dignity and social justice are divine norms is rooted in the Old Testament law.

The New Testament brings freedom and love together even more radically. The New Testament proclaims that Christ's forgiveness has set us free, that we have been accepted as we are, and that we are now liberated from all rules and regulations. Freedom in Christ is not freedom to sin, however, but to live in the Spirit—that is, we are free to love others as God has loved us in Jesus Christ. There are no limits to what love may call us to do. There is no rule that specifies how much we should share, after which we might rest satisfied with ourselves. Love without limits might lead to suffering, or even death, as it did for Christ himself.

So if Christians live in the Spirit, they should embody the best intentions of both the Left and Right. They have been given the liberty of sons of God, free from all legalism, earthly authority, and fear. They know that before the Father they are equal with all other people. And they have as their example the fraternal loyalty of their Lord, who suffered and died for the sake of humanity.

Christians should, therefore, transcend the particular societies in which they live. In this regard, we might learn from Christians in Communist countries. Simply to be a Christian in a Communist country is a continuing protest for personal liberty, against the state and its ideology. Pope John Paul II, particularly during his visit to Poland, has made the world more aware of the role of churches in Communist countries and their service in defense of human rights.

East German church people have coined the phrase *critical solidarity* to describe their stance in a Communist society. At an ecumenical conference in France several years ago, I met an East German pastor who exemplified critical solidarity. He could have moved to the West in the first years after the Second World War, but decided to stay in his parish. This conference was his first trip outside East Europe in twenty years. He praised his government's achievements in leveling class differences and providing for the poor, but quietly—fearfully—opposed their dictatorial methods and harassment of the church. His children had not been allowed to enter the university because of their faith, a real loss to a family which had always valued education highly. They had become tradesmen instead and, partly to compensate for the loss of university studies, had become accomplished amateur musicians. One son was a prayer-meeting leader, and their gatherings had recently been graced by speaking in tongues. I was delighted to learn that the charismatic movement had spread to East Germany, because it dramatizes the Spirit's spontaneity and God's transcendence to Christians in a country desperately in need of both.

For many Christians in Communist countries, dissent has been even more costly. Albania's Party has been one of the most vicious, but the story of Shtjefen Kurti, shot to death in 1973, could be repeated for hundreds of other contemporary martyrs in Communist countries:

> Father Kurti was in fact first sentenced to death in 1945, having been charged with "spying for the Vatican." This sentence was commuted to life imprisonment, and 18 years later he was released from prison. He then returned to parish work, but when the government declared all religious practices to be illegal he took a secular job as a clerk in a cooperative. Soon after this soldiers arrived to destroy Father Kurti's parish church, and he fought them with his fists. For this offence he was sentenced to a further sixteen years' imprisonment, but he continued to exercise his priesthood secretly, and during the early part of 1973 a woman prisoner asked him to baptize her child. The ceremony took place privately, but news of it reached the authorities who once again put the 70-year-old priest on trial and later handed him over to a military firing squad. He was said to have been found guilty of "subversive activities" designed to overthrow the State.[13]

From this example Christians in capitalist countries might take some courage for *critical solidarity* in our societies. We can be grateful for the liberty we enjoy, but must dissent from the inequality and segregation by race and income which often characterize capitalist societies.

We can begin our dissent from the self-centered ethos of capitalism by giving away time and money to voluntary organizations or to individuals in need. The traditional tithe is good self-discipline. We can approach daily tasks with honesty and charity; in almost any job we can be of real service, doing even tedious tasks with diligence and a sense of broader purpose. We can spend time with children and direct them toward service. We can pray for the Spirit's guidance in making major decisions: we can look for more than beauty or affluence when we are thinking about marrying someone; we can consider risky or mixed neighborhoods when we are buying a home; and we can count service more important than income or prestige in planning a career.

Much of the freedom of the West is wasted. Too many people trudge ahead in bland, consumerist conformity, taking whatever jobs pay best or buying the most expensive houses they can. Even Christian congregations often serve themselves first, budgeting their funds to air-condition their buildings, educate their children, and recruit their affluent neighbors.

Could Christians, at least, be genuinely free? Could we more often depart from "successful" career paths, opt not to buy things which others consider "essential," or involve ourselves in unfashionable social commitments? Might more Christians opt for voluntary poverty, perhaps living in supportive communities, in order to be more fully of service to people in need?

In my own city, Washington, D.C., a group called the Community for Creative Non-Violence opens its doors to people in need—whoever happens to come in off the street. They have frequently been engaged in protests and demonstrations on behalf of the poor. The Community operates a daily soup kitchen for the indigent. They are like a Roman Catholic religious order in some ways, but they are an ecumenical community, and members commit themselves for different periods of time. Their communalism recalls that of the first church in Jerusalem, and their voluntary poverty makes them available to poor people in a total and personal way which my more affluent life-style, for example, precludes.

Most people, also Christians, will probably continue to conform more closely to the affluent life-styles we have come to consider normal. But, as I suggested in the last chapter, time and energy we are now spending in unsatisfying ways can be freed for other purposes, if we are at all open to God. Now I am suggesting that, if we are at all open to God, they will be shared with others who suffer from the inequities and cruelties of capitalistic society.

Our time and energy can be shared directly and personally or, sometimes with more effect, channeled into political action to reform society at large. Ever since capitalism began, some Christians have been active in reforming its negative aspects. As industrialization proceeded in the nineteenth century, reform became as much a part of Anglo-American Protestantism as was revival, and the historic concern of the Roman Catholic Church can be traced in a series of papal encyclicals on social questions.[14]

During this century the World Council of Churches and the Vatican have been more and more vocal and, at times, radical in their commitments. In the United States Martin Luther King exemplified Christian political ministry, and the anti-war movement drew much of its strength from the churches (particularly before and after the draft recruited millions of young men and their friends into its ranks). In Latin America the church has been in the forefront of the democratic, reformist resistance against a number of Right-wing regimes (such as in El Salvador, Chile, and Brazil), and many Latin American theologians are writing that the best way to understand God in Latin America is through participation in the struggles against social injustice.[15] Scores of Christians have been put in prison or exiled because of prophetic words about injustice in Right-wing Asian countries (such as South Korea and the Philippines) and under the racist regimes of southern Africa.

Christians will take many different positions on political issues, of course. Their information, their opinions on the merits of markets versus planning, and their moral judgments on political questions will all vary. Many Christians might agree, however, on five generalizations:

1. Both the Right and Left in modern politics are grounded in values we share, and we are glad for modern efforts, by all parties, to mold society in accordance with ethical principles.

2. Neither unrestrained capitalism nor totalitarian socialism is ethically attractive. Compromise systems—a reforming capitalism or democratic socialism—make sense. The United States probably still has much to learn from the more socially developed nations of Western Europe. As capitalist countries move slowly toward the Left, and Communist countries become less Stalinist, one can hope for some convergence of the two systems.

3. The world remains broken. We have not devised ethically adequate institutions. We must make tough, ambiguous choices, weighing the practical and moral results of various half-measures and more or less satisfactory solutions. We may, in various situations, opt for capitalist, socialist, or compromise solutions.

4. Different countries need different solutions. A middle-income country with sharp class divisions may require drastic state action in favor of the poor, while a very low-income country with inefficient public administration might benefit if state intervention and regulation were reduced. What works in a relatively homogenous, closely-knit country like Sweden may not work in a huge, diverse country like the United States, and what makes sense in the United States

may well not make sense in countries with much less income or different cultural backgrounds.

5. For those of us who live in capitalistic, individualistic societies like the United States, the critique from the Left at least provides a compelling agenda of concerns: poverty, racism, sexism, inadequate public services (schools, health care, public transportation), weak macroeconomic control (inflation and unemployment), and abuses of private power and wealth.

5

One World:
Rich and Poor

WORLD POVERTY

In evaluating urban projects for the World Bank, I have estimated the extent of poverty in a number of cities in East Africa and Latin America. I found that in the towns of Botswana roughly 40% of families probably cannot afford a calorie-adequate diet. In Tanzania the figure was nearly 50%; in Addis Ababa, Ethiopia, about 65%. Even in Guayaquil, Ecuador, booming and relatively prosperous, an estimated 37% of families are unable to afford a calorie-adequate diet. These estimates ignore all considerations of quality such as protein. They are based on the starchy diet poor people eat and the percentage of income they normally spend for food. Few of these underfed people are obviously dying of hunger, but their babies are born small; many of their children die of diseases complicated by underfeeding and malnourishment; and of those who survive, some never achieve their genetic potential either physically or mentally.

Nobody knows with any accuracy, but perhaps 800 million people worldwide, in both urban and rural areas, are absolutely poor, their *basic needs* for food, shelter, health, and education unmet.[1]

Kurt Waldheim, Secretary-General of the United Nations, rightly called mass poverty "the single most devastating indictment of current world civilization." *The extent of absolute poverty is intolerable.*

Over the last generation the developing countries have, on the whole, achieved growth in per capita income at about the same rates as the developed countries, but the *gap* between rich and poor countries has widened.[2] This is because of the tremendous initial disparity. If a relatively wealthy country has $3000 in GNP per capita per year, compared to $300 GNP per capita in a poor country, and if the poor country manages to match the rich country's growth at, say, 5% per year, at the end of one year the rich country's income would be $3,150, that of the poor country $315. Despite the economic achievement of the poor country, the gap between them would have widened by $135.

Some developing countries have, in fact, grown faster in percentage terms than the developed countries. A few industrializing countries, like Brazil and Korea, are catching up with the older industrialized countries, and there has been a drastic shift of the world's wealth toward the oil-producing countries. On the other hand, a group of about 50 nations, now among the poorest in the world, have grown very slowly, falling far behind the developed and faster growing developing countries. Moreover, the distribution of income within many developing countries is more skewed than it was a generation ago.[3]

In the course of my work I associate with people at all levels of the world's income distribution. I usually live in Washington, D.C., sharing in its convenience and affluence. Nearly a third of the year, however, I work in developing countries, sharing the problems of government officials who are trying to introduce reforms into situations where few things change quickly. My government colleagues are usually underpaid, certainly in comparison to wages in the United States.

And then we visit urban slums where many families survive without adequate food. Many children do not attend school, and, if they do, their classrooms are crowded and the teachers poorly trained. Crowded neighborhoods may do without bus service for lack of passable streets. Diarrhea and more serious diseases are endemic because clean water and sewage disposal may not be available.

These gaps in the world's income distribution are one reason for some people's frustration with economic development. Such frustration is widespread in Latin America, for example, despite rapid economic growth, because of the continuing contrast with U.S. affluence nearby and a widening gap between rich and poor within countries. *The contrast between the world's rich and poor mocks all sentiments of human brotherhood.*

The moral problem of world poverty is aggravated by a history of *exploitation*. Most developing countries probably benefited, on balance, from their contacts with richer countries, but imperialist policies consistently favored the imperial powers.

Modern imperialism began with European crusades and early colonial ventures for booty. By the eighteenth century the goal of exploitation had changed: European nations managed colonies abroad to provide cheap raw materials (including slave labor) and markets for manufactured goods. In the nineteenth century colonialism expanded militarily; it was the era of the conquest of Africa, the dismemberment of China, and U.S. military impositions around the Caribbean. By then some industrial powers, notably England and the United States, found it to their advantage to advocate

free trade. But the prejudicial pattern of colonial development continued, with the colonies encouraged to rely on
one or two crops or mineral resources for their exports,
and their industrial development discouraged.

Over the last generation Europe's former colonies in
Asia and Africa have seized independence, and Latin
American nations have reasserted their independence from
U.S. influence. Decolonization continues to make news:
Black-majority rule in Zimbabwe-Rhodesia, violence in
Indochina after wars with France and the United States,
charges that Israel and Taiwan are colonial creations,
change and revolution in Central America. The imbalance
in world power continues, and many representatives of the
developing countries claim that the rich countries continue
to manipulate world politics and the rules of the world
economy to their own advantage. *Undoubtedly, the richer
countries have often taken unfair advantage of the poorer
countries.*

Absolute poverty keeps millions of people from developing their God-given potential. The wide divergence between
rich and poor, internationally and within countries, invites
eventual violence. And the rich normally watch out for their
own interests at the expense of the poor. For these three
reasons world poverty is, except for the danger of nuclear
war, the most pressing ethical issue of the generation.

The moral imperative of doing something about the
problem of world poverty is generally recognized. This
consensus is grounded on the three values of economic
culture which are almost unanimously shared in the council
of nations: *this-worldly* prosperity is important; *progress* toward it is possible everywhere; and it can be achieved
through *rational* reform and improved technology.

Some of the frustration on both sides of relations between
rich and poor countries is also related to fundamental mod-

ern values. The tension within the Enlightenment family of social values, discussed in Chapter 4, also complicates relations between rich and poor nations. It underlies the tension between two important trends in relations between rich and poor nations—the trend toward world unity and the trend away from colonialism.

WORLD UNITY AND NATIONALISM

Increasing world interdependence and anti-colonial nationalism are perhaps the two most influential forces shaping relations between richer and poorer nations.

Increasing world interdependence is a matter of fact:

• There are hardly any isolated cultures anymore. You can go virtually anywhere and speak at least one of the old imperial languages—English, French, or Spanish. Structures of government, some customs, and even structures of thought are similar from one country to another.

• When peasants in Bangladesh listen to world news on their shortwave radios, they hear much of the same news we see on television. They know about our elections and fads, and when disaster strikes, we actually look them in the face through television.

• A round-the-world trip costs much less than a new car. One in 85 U.S. citizens is living abroad, and you can find people from other countries in any medium-sized U.S. town.[4]

The unity we experience, however, is not primarily based on bonds of mutual concern. It has been forged by conquest, trade, and technology. The great empires of the European states brought virtually the entire world together by force, and colonial subjects were often excluded from positions of respect unless they learned the language and aped the culture of the Europeans. New technologies—airplanes and radios—have tied the poor even more closely to

faraway places and to changes they may not fully understand, let alone control.

As the influence of the West began to reach into East
Europe and then Asia and Africa, each new Western-edu-
cated intelligensia wavered between assimilation and tra-
ditionalism. Each "backward" people was stung by jibes
and held back by discrimination. *Nationalism* allowed them
to strike back against oppression, reassert national worth,
and, at the same time, struggle for modernization.

Nationalism has spread throughout the world over the
last 200 years along with—and in reaction to—economic development and increasing world unity. In a world of un-
even economic development, anti-colonial nationalism has
provided a series of locks through which peoples can move
deliberately, maintaining independence and dignity, on
their way toward prosperity. Without nationalism the
white rich would dominate the world much more thoroughly than they do now.[5]

Starting in about 1955 with the Bandung Conference of
Non-Aligned Nations, many of the newly independent
countries began to organize as a separate bloc. They were
called the Third World, because they refused to be identi-
fied with either the "free world" or the "Communist
world." [6] In recent years, the Third World is sometimes
called the South, as distinguished from the wealthier capitalist and Communist countries of the North; this termi-
nology, too, conveys the determination of many developing
nations to struggle together for self-determination and a
greater share of the world's prosperity. They are a diverse
bloc, including all kinds of cultures, political systems, and
levels of economic development, united only by the shared
experience of relative poverty and powerlessness over
against the richer, industrialized countries. The bloc has
gained clout with the successes of OPEC, holding together
despite the crippling impact of higher oil prices on the

non-OPEC developing countries, partly because the OPEC countries have been generous in foreign aid (giving away about six times the proportion of GNP which the industrialized countries give).[7]

Radical analysts doubt that negotiations for a new world order between local elites and international capitalism are likely to benefit the poor. They argue for revolution in the Third World, overthrowing local elites and more completely disengaging from international capitalism. They point to countries like the People's Republic of China as models of socialist development based on economic independence.

The ethical importance of increasing world interdependence is obvious to everyone. It is a practical realization of the age-old vision of worldwide *fraternity*. But, since ethics tend to be tailored to self-interest, people in the rich countries sometimes fail to appreciate the moral legitimacy of Third World nationalism. Third World nationalism is a protest for *liberty* and *equality* among nations. The anti-colonial movement has claimed the right of each people to run its own affairs and to have a fair share of the world's wealth and power.

Growing world interdependence and Third World nationalism can be viewed as one dynamic, both motivated by fundamental ethical principles which are, ultimately, in harmony. Over the medium term, however, interdependence and nationalism are often in tension.

Some developing countries experience this tension in their efforts to be thoroughly independent and also narrow the economic gap which divides them from the rich. In the early years of political independence in Asia and Africa it seemed plausible that economic self-reliance might be the quickest route to economic growth. The Soviet Union and Japan had both put themselves into the club of the rich by developing in relative isolation.

But a generation later it is clear that the biggest economic payoff from nationalism has been for the resource-rich countries, notably OPEC members, who have established their rights to manage and price the resources within their boundaries. Models of self-reliant industrialization based on the experiences of the Soviet Union and Japan have only worked, and there only to some extent, in large and relatively well-administered countries like China and India. Smaller, poorer countries which have opted for self-reliance have, by and large, suffered slower growth. I think of self-reliant Tanzania in contrast to Kenya, isolationist Burma in contrast to Malaysia, or Jamaica in contrast to Bermuda. Similarly, the tariff barriers many Latin American countries erected to protect domestic industries probably slowed their economic growth.

When Ghana achieved independence in 1957, its new prime minister, Kwame Nkrumah, made a wager with Felix Houphouet-Boigny, who was to become president of neighboring Ivory Coast.* They reportedly made a bet on which country, similar in resources but pursuing contrasting policies, would be richer after ten years. Ivory Coast became independent at a later date; Africans continued to work for Europeans in many businesses; and there are still some cafes and hotels in its capital city which few Africans can afford. Ghana broke colonial ties earlier and opted for a more self-reliant economy. There were few foreigners in Ghana, even fewer in positions of authority. But Nkrumah was deposed before the ten years were over, and he should have paid Houphouet. Africans in the Ivory Coast were visibly richer at the end of the decade than their counterparts in more self-reliant Ghana, and the difference continues to widen.

In some situations economic independence is worth the risk of slower growth. Blacks in the Republic of South Africa enjoy higher levels of material consumption than

Africans in any of the independent Black African nations, but what material benefits could justify the humiliation and subjugation they suffer in South Africa? Zambia chose to eject most of the white settlers who were in their country before independence, perhaps at some economic cost, but as Zambia's president, Kenneth Kaunda, has written:

> Efficiency cannot be measured wholly or even chiefly in terms of results that can be reduced to quantifiable terms. . . . The winning of power by the people to do things for themselves and to run their own affairs produces results in terms of dignity and human self-fulfillment which remain things of profound importance in terms of the quality of life our people live.[9]

Many intellectuals in Latin America, including the "liberation theologians," are convinced that economic growth is less important to their countries than breaking old patterns of domination and dependence. Some say that dependence is culturally and psychologically debilitating:

> The world's rich "discovered," invaded, subjugated, governed, converted, educated, criticized, and now aid the Third World. What is called "underdevelopment" is at its deepest root a prostration of the spirit.[10]

Others argue that it will be necessary to break ties with rich foreigners to achieve more democracy and needed social reforms. They see that multinational corporations (aided, on occasion even militarily, by the U.S. government) often join forces with domestic groups who oppose popular political movements, because instability is bad for business and might lead to their own expropriation.

There seem to be limits to how much interaction with the outside world different peoples or cultures can sustain. Korea, for example, seems to be able to open itself almost completely to foreign influence without losing its cultural self-confidence. One can think of numerous countries, however, especially in Africa, where foreign influence has led to a weakening of traditional values, to opportunism, and to political corruption. The post-Shah backlash against foreign influence in Iran is evidence that, among other abuses, the Shah's regime probably overstepped the limits of how much foreign presence the people of Iran wanted to withstand.

My point here is only that developing countries are having to make tough choices between economic nationalism and the advantages of integration with the expanding world economy. They have good reasons for wanting more independence. But if they choose to run their own affairs, somewhat isolated from the manipulations of the rich, they risk getting left behind economically.

The rich countries also experience tension between growing world interdependence and Third World nationalism. The rich countries are generally eager for increasing world unity. It is economically beneficial to them, too, and they are usually the dominant "partner" in relations with developing countries. Third World nationalism, on the other hand, sometimes gets in the way of closer relations. It sets up barriers, and it leads to annoying claims on the wealth and privileges of the more developed nations.

The convergence of growing world unity and anticolonialism poses a challenge to the richer nations. This was clearly stated by the Sixth Special Session of the United Nations General Assembly in its historic Declaration for a New International Economic Order. The Declaration began in praise of Third World nationalism:

> The greatest and most significant achievement during the last decades has been the independence from colonial and alien domination of a large number of peoples and nations.

It continued with a description of growing world interdependence:

> [Changes in the world economy since 1970] have thrust into prominence the reality of interdependence of all the members of the world community. Current events have brought into sharp focus the realization that the interests of the developed countries and those of the developing countries can no longer be isolated from each other, . . . and that the prosperity of the international community as a whole depends upon the prosperity of its constituent parts.[11]

The Assembly agreed that these two world-shaping movements, toward interdependence and away from colonialism, could not both continue without a restructuring of the world economy to allow increased self-determination and prosperity to the developing nations. The New International Economic Order would require nonreciprocal concessions from the richer nations. It would be in the long-run interest of the richer nations to negotiate a New International Economic Order, however, because of their increasing vulnerability to the Third World (their need for oil, other minerals, and export markets in the Third World).

I think this logic is correct. But even if the natural resources, growing economic clout, and political power of the Third World were not enough to convince the rich countries to make concessions, Christians in the rich countries should be working for a New International Economic Order anyway. The anticolonial movement's protest against *imperialistic* world unity is ethically correct. It insists on liberty and equality among peoples, as well as fraternity. Can fraternity ever be based on the domination of the poor by the rich? Genuine fraternity implies liberty and equality as well—at the international level, a community of free and equal peoples.

A broad range of specific ways in which the spirit of

anticolonialism might influence the structures of world interdependence are being discussed in international forums under the banner of a New International Economic Order: [12]

1. **Aid.** Will the rich nations increase foreign aid, or will aid continue to average less than a third of one percent of their national incomes? Will more aid be "untied" from the commercial and foreign policy interests of the rich countries? Will the World Bank's capacity to loan to middle-income countries and grant low-interest loans to low-income countries be expanded?

2. **Trade.** Will the richer countries lower tariffs and relax quotas on imports, particularly manufactured goods, from the developing countries? Will the Common Fund be big and flexible enough to effectively stabilize commodity prices and export earnings? More controversially, should price support be introduced for some Third World exports?

3. **Debt.** Will the capacity of the International Monetary Fund be expanded to help countries adjust to repeated oil price increases? Will the developed countries forgive past debts for the poorer developing countries?

4. **Multinational corporations.** Can a code of conduct for multinationals be agreed? Should nations have the right, by international law, to nationalize foreign business interests without compensation?

5. **International institutions.** Should developing countries have more say in the governance of the World Bank and International Monetary Fund? Should UNCTAD (United Nations Conference on Trade and Development), in which the developing countries dominate, rather than GATT (General Agreement on Tariffs and Trade), in which the industrialized countries dominate, become the primary forum for negotiating international trade issues?

6. **Media.** How can press coverage of the developing countries be improved and balanced by media owned and operated in the Third World?

7. **Seabed.** Can we devise rules for the exploitation of resources under the sea that would combine private initiative and efficiency with public regulation and benefit?

8. **Science and technology.** How can more research be directed toward development needs, rather than defense or luxury? Should developing countries have access to technologies which are patented by private business in the developed countries?

9. **Food.** Will national and international grain reserves be established and maintained at levels which would preclude world shortages?

Some changes have already been negotiated, many of them measures (like trade liberalization or adjustments to higher oil prices) which almost immediately benefit the richer countries as well as the poorer countries. Further deals can be negotiated between the developed and developing countries simply on the basis of mutual self-interest, but as Theodore Hesburgh and James Grant wrote in their preface to the Overseas Development Council's *United States and World Development Agenda* for 1979:

> Successful North-South cooperation on mutually beneficial "packages" of international economic issues probably will not be possible without the motivating force of a larger, common purpose to which all subscribe.[13]

Official negotiations between North and South have been characterized by considerable hostile rhetoric from the South, some intransigence on the part of the North, and less reform than would be in everyone's interest. To break this deadlock in official negotiations, Robert McNamara, president of the World Bank, invited Willy Brandt, Nobel Peace Prize winner and former chancellor of West Germany, to assemble an unofficial commission of distinguished citizens from all over the world. In 1980 the Brandt Commission published its report on international development issues, titled *North-South: A Proposal for Survival* (MIT Press). The report is eminently practical. It highlights mutually beneficial packages of reforms, recommending, for example, aid for energy exploration, both to raise incomes for developing countries and to lower energy prices for developed countries. But it sets such specific deals between North and South within the context of the "larger, common purpose" to which Hesburgh and Grant alluded. If our interdependent world is to survive, the Brandt Commission claims, it must become a more just world.

As I read their report, I hear echoes of the Old Testament prophets telling ancient Israel that the nation could not, in the long term, be secure without justice. To interpret the Brandt Commission's message in the terms of this chapter: the international *fraternity* which technology and commerce have established cannot, in the long term, survive if it does not foster *liberty* and *equality* among nations as well.

Does it help to note the basic values which underlie the historic movements which shape North-South relations? As in the case of the capitalism–socialism debate, a careful look at underlying values may allow us to grasp the ultimate harmony of two opposing movements. It may keep us from a self-interested, one-sided consistency.

In addition, thinking about the ethical mainsprings of demands for a New International Economic Order suggests a bargain which rich countries might strike with the governments of developing countries: the industrialized nations will move toward a New International Economic Order, if the developing nations move toward a new internal order within the borders.[14] The bargain would be hypocritical unless people in the developed countries also become more concerned about poverty at home, and it should not be used to justify neocolonial interferences in the domestic affairs of the developing countries. But the bargain makes sense.

If rich countries are being asked to make concessions for the sake of nationalist liberty and international fraternity, can they not ask the leadership of the developing countries to be more concerned about the liberty of their own citizens and to make sure that poor people have a share in development?

Such a bargain is not a new suggestion. It represents a trend in dealings between rich and poor countries. President Carter made basic human rights a prominent concern of U.S. foreign policy, and foreign aid in the 1970s was directed more toward projects of specific benefit to poor people. It is a trend worth continuing. The ethical analogy between poor nations within the world and poor people within developing countries lends credibility to it.

WHAT CAN WE DO?

All this seems remote from the lives of most individuals. High moral principles are not worth much unless people can put them into practice. Some Christians are ready to make changes in their lives, and some church groups are ready to reorient their programs to address the problem of world poverty. But what can individuals or private groups in the rich countries do that will make much difference to poor people abroad? (My focus here is on people in the rich countries, because, due to language barriers and the way book-marketing works, I assume most of my readers will be in the United States.)

There is, in fact, little that individuals or private groups can do by themselves if they are far away from poor people in the Third World. World poverty is a massive international challenge, and the contributions that people in the United States can make will be primarily *political*.

It might be more satisfying if all of us could assist the poor abroad personally. We would enjoy some unam-

biguously helpful act, preferably as intimate as television
has made our awareness of poverty abroad. Some of the
largest voluntary development agencies are those which
place "tearful child" advertisements and arrange for personal communication between a "foster child" abroad and
his U.S. donor. These agencies present an unrepresenta-
tive picture of developing countries, and the administrative
costs of such person-to-person programs are high. They
are popular, however, because they claim to offer opportunities for international relations as personal as giving to a
neighbor in need.

Attempts to link simpler life-styles to world hunger have
a similar appeal. They offer something I can do on my own
to help the world's poor. It feels good and right. But do
simpler life-styles really help poor people abroad?

• Some writers have urged concerned people to lower
their consumption of food, by eating less meat for example,
in order to leave more food for the world's poor.[15] The
effect of eating less meat, however, would be to lower
agricultural prices. Farmers and ranchers would react by
producing less. Poor people could gain slightly from lower
prices, but the affluent would lose much more than the poor
would gain. If eating less meat makes me, let us say, 1%
less affluent, I would help the poor more by giving away
1% of my income to an agency involved with the poor
abroad, spending the remainder however I like.

• Charles Elliot, a theologian-economist associated with
the World Council of Churches, argues that the Golden
Rule implies that we should not live more affluently than
everyone in the world could conceivably live. Ron Sider,
author of *Rich Christians in an Age of Hunger,* tells how his
family, following this kind of logic, painfully reduced their
consumption to $7000 a year.[16] In itself, however, reducing
consumption does not help the poor. Spending less on fine
arts, for example, would result in the loss of some things

of beauty, but would do nothing to help the poor. Mass reductions in overall consumption would, in fact, harm the world's poor. The worst times in developing countries are when demand is slack in the rich countries.

• A more genuine link between modest life-styles and world poverty is the scarcity of irreplaceable resources—oil and coal, perhaps minerals, the ecosphere. If we do not conserve these resources, we may not only spoil the world for our children, but make it impossible for people from developing countries to ever enjoy them. This argument is somewhat speculative, however.[17] I expect that existing resources, along with technological innovations, will allow gradual increases in standards of living worldwide into the foreseeable future.[18] If innovations in energy technology do not begin to appear after some years of intensified research, more drastic reductions in our consumption of nonreplaceable resources would become more clearly appropriate.

I agree that U.S. life-styles, including common eating habits, are wasteful and self-destructive. I agree that more modest life-styles may be symbolically important, as a sign of solidarity with the poor. I appreciate the efforts some people are making to reduce their consumption, especially of nonreplaceable resources. But such changes will help the world's poor significantly only if they free time and money which are then *spent for the direct benefit of the poor.*

There are a few ways for individuals to become directly involved. They might give assistance to foreign students in the United States, or take jobs in government, the churches, or universities which would involve them full-time in the quest for a more just world order.[19] A few may decide to seek out service opportunities for themselves in developing countries—in voluntary organizations, international organizations, government, business, or education. In order to assist such people Elizabeth Anne Donnelly and I compiled a comprehensive guide entitled *The Overseas List: Opportunities for Living and Working in Developing Countries* (Augsburg, 1979).

People can also join forces with other concerned individuals in supporting voluntary organizations involved in development work abroad. Catholic Relief Service and CARE are the biggest of these organizations; they do important work well. The denominational agencies, like Lutheran World Relief, are competent too, and some of the smaller organizations—like the Mennonite Central Committee, American Friends Service Committee, and Volunteers in Technical Assistance—are particularly creative. The better missionary organizations—Maryknoll, for example, or the American Lutheran Church—sponsor personalized development work in conjunction with evangelism.[20]

Ron Sider argues for much more private sharing, partly to add credibility to our lobbying for public change:

> Central to any Christian strategy on world hunger must be a radical call for the Church to be the Church. One of the glaring weaknesses of the churches' social action in the past few decades is that . . . the Church concentrated too exclusively on political solutions. In effect, Church leaders tried to persuade government to legislate what they could not persuade their Church members to live. And politicians quickly sensed that the daring declarations and frequent Washington delegations represented generals without troops. Only if the body of Christ is already beginning to live a radically new model of economic sharing will our demand for political change have integrity and impact.[21]

Political action is essential, however. Private efforts of charity are simply dwarfed by the broader relationships between the developed and developing countries. We drink coffee picked in El Salvador, burn oil from the Middle East, and walk on carpets backed by jute from Bangladesh. My savings account at a local bank may allow it to buy bonds from Chase Manhattan Bank, which in turn may have loaned the funds to Peru. Our taxes finance U.S. foreign policy initiatives around the world, foreign aid, and the production of arms for sale or grant to developing countries.

How significant are our charities in comparison to these broader relationships with the developing countries? All the U.S. voluntary agencies together now spend about $1 billion a year for aid to Israel and the developing countries. All U.S. churches together may spend another $1 billion for evangelistic mission abroad.[22] By contrast, trade between developing and developed countries in 1976 amounted to about $200 billion, [23] and foreign investment in the developing countries amounted to about $46 billion.[24] Representatives of the developing countries have proposed that these major relationships between them and us be somewhat restructured to their benefit.

Thus the importance of organizations like Bread for the World, the Christian citizens' movement. Formed in the early 1970s, Bread for the World organizes Christians of all denominations by congressional district to lobby for changes in the interest of the poor. Living in Washington, I am especially aware of the hundreds of well-funded lobbies here that watch out for the interests of all sorts of groups. Bread for the World members contact their representatives in government about specific legislative and administrative actions which might benefit people who do not have enough food. A book entitled *Bread for the World* (Paulist and Eerdmans, 1975) written by Arthur Simon, the organization's executive director, outlines their general understanding of issues related to world hunger.

It might be possible to overcome the worst aspects of world poverty by the year 2000. Meeting that target, however, would require a movement of concern in the United

States. The movement would need the vigor of support for the Marshall Plan in the early 1950s or the civil rights and antiwar movements of the 1960s. No such movement is stirring, however. On the contrary, the dominant movement in U.S. politics is toward fiscal conservatism, except for military measures to bolster national security. The opportunity to bolster long-term security by an all-out effort to overcome world poverty is being largely ignored.

If the churches are to play their part in giving ethical shape to the world economy, Christians must, first, learn to include world poverty more prominently in their prayers, counting it among their fundamental and abiding concerns. Second, we need more ecclesiastical and para-ecclesiastical organizations (like the Maryknoll Missioners and Bread for the World) to study development issues in ethical perspective and formulate various courses of action. Finally, we need more Christians who, despite the tediousness of politics and the complexity of this problem, are willing to become involved in the international politics of alleviating world poverty. Through prayer, study, and organization, Christians might be able to make the ideals of liberty, equality, and fraternity seem a little less hollow in this divided world.

6

Evangelism
for Development?

If world poverty is to be overcome, it is not enough that the rich repent or that a New International Economic Order be established. Development is associated with economic culture, a particular set of values which challenge long-held traditions and fundamental beliefs, especially among the world's poor. The hard truth is that the poor themselves will have to change too, if they are to participate more fully in modern prosperity.

All the traditional religions of the world, like Christianity, are in tension with modern economic culture. In the West, Christianity has been under attack and in a process of reform for several centuries. The crisis of conscience is thus more acute in developing countries, especially among the poor.

Is economic development worth culture change? What, specifically, is at issue between the world's great living religions and economic culture? In what ways is culture change coming about, and what is the role of Christian mission?

These are far-reaching questions, and anyone's answers must be tentative. But, based on some years of reflection and study, I make a series of three arguments in this chapter:

1. Economic development is better than poverty by almost any culture's standards.

2. The culture associated with economic development is in tension with all the traditional religions.

3. Christian evangelism can contribute to humane economic development.

This chain of argument is *not*, in any way, intended to suggest that people should become Christians because it pays. First, just because economic development is good, that does not mean it is the *only* good, nor that people should compromise what they consider true and right for the sake of material growth. Second, the tension between religions and economic culture cuts two ways, the world's religions challenged by economic culture, but also challenging simplistic secularist assumptions.[1] And third, the Christian "materialism" outlined in Chapters 2 and 3 would, in any case, be relatively austere in comparison to the consumerist bonanza of crass materialism.

IS DEVELOPMENT WORTH CULTURE CHANGE?

The opinion is sometimes expressed, particularly in the rich countries, that economic development is an imposition on people of other cultures, that they would be better off to avoid the problems which modernity brings. Since each religion or culture has its own values, why encourage economic values? Poor peoples around the world are scrambling to raise their incomes and enjoy the benefits of modernity, but they, too, sometimes have second thoughts about what they are leaving behind in the process.

There are costs to any change, but economic development does tend to improve many aspects of the quality of life.

Certain things—like happiness, health, beauty, truth, security, communion with God, and morality—are highly valued in virtually all cultures. Different cultures have their own styles of art and music, but people who are recognized for their good taste in one culture have been shown to be able to distinguish good from bad in the art of another culture.[2] Mankind does not agree on what the truth is, but ignorance is everywhere recognized, also by the ignorant, for what it is. Social structure varies, but every society encourages morality, justice, and internal peace. Societies war against each other, but each wants security from external attack. Nearly everyone would like to be reconciled to the principalities and powers behind nature and history, although some think there are many gods and some that there is no God at all.

What is the effect of development in terms of these qualities of life which are almost universally considered worthwhile?

Happiness. There are at least three different feelings we call "happiness." First, there is the temporary feeling we get when we meet or exceed our expectations. It is an emotional barometer, indicating changes in our welfare from moment to moment. People who normally have less tend to be, in this sense, happy with less.

A second sort of happiness—contentment—depends on inner spiritual resources. Maybe people swept up in the materialistic bustle—calculating, planning, dependent on huge and hectic institutions—are more liable to anxiety about tomorrow's bread, less able to relax with the sparrows and lilies of the field.

Whether or not people in rich societies are more or less anxious hour by hour, they may, however, be happier in a third sense. They may be more satisfied with their lot in life when they pause to reflect. This point is debatable, but at least Gallup's first global public opinion poll found that, on the average, people from the richer countries—those who live in North America, Australia, and Western Europe—report themselves as being happier, find their lives more interesting, worry less, and would like fewer changes in their existence. They are also more satisfied with their family life, their countries, their communities, their education, and themselves. By contrast, only 28% of the Latin Americans, 8% of the Africans, and 6% of the Indians interviewed considered themselves fully satisfied with their lives.[3] Another, older cross-cultural study reported somewhat higher levels of satisfaction in wealthier nations, although the differences in satisfaction were not nearly as great as the differences in income.[4]

Health. The very poor are enervated by parasites and sometimes permanently stupified by malnutrition. Hard labor may make them handsome in youth, but disease soon leaves its scars, and death often comes prematurely.

Beauty. Anyone can enjoy natural beauties, and the poorest people deck their bodies with pretty things, their spirits with tales and songs. But folk art often lacks the materials, time, and expertise required for great art.

Truth and justice. Since most of the poor cannot read or write, or make any but the most elementary arithmetical calculations, they are unable to analyze their own situations adequately. They are also vulnerable to the wiles of richer, better educated neighbors; it is almost impossible to establish social justice as long as the poor are unable to fend for themselves.

Security. Similarly, poor nations are less able to repel foreign aggression.

Religion. The poor are not even able to understand very much about religion, although they may especially love God and He them. We have all met poor people who inspire us by their piety and charity, but knowledge is also an important aspect of religious life, and the poor, who often cannot afford education, are especially vulnerable to superstition and narrow-mindedness.

Morality. On this final and crucial point, the results of economic development are ambiguous. I don't so much bemoan the fact that development may undermine the discipline of traditional communities. The mores of tribes and small towns can be dangerously arbitrary and parochial. The ethical standards associated with wealth, particularly the values of economic culture, are more universal and reliable. But modern, wealthy people are perhaps less faithful to these ethical principles than poorer peoples are to their less sophisticated principles, and twisted affluence can do more damage—in war, for example—than the perversities of the poor.

In summary, economic development does not make people less sinful, but it does tend toward satisfaction, health, beauty, truth, justice, and increased power for good or ill— cogent arguments in favor of change for people from almost any cultural or religious background.

Thinking like this can easily degenerate into cultural imperiousness, so I want to couch my claims for cultural change with a number of warnings.

First, all peoples are essentially equal, regardless of material achievement. That is a God-given principle, apprehended by faith. Regardless of wealth or poverty, we should, for God's sake, approach other peoples with respect, assuming their good sense and ready to learn from them. We should be humbled by our own ignorance, by our inclination to reject strange customs and ridicule what we do not understand. We should treat all people as sisters and brothers, equally loved by the Father, even if everyone is not equally well-schooled or skilled.

Second, each culture bears unique gifts of beauty and

wisdom. Even poor people enjoy all life's basic joys, and
the poorest human being is highly sophisticated and accomplished. Some primitive peoples, especially before much
contact with modern civilization, are exceptionally com-
munal and content. Their ability to cope with natural adversity, the simplicity of their lives, and the intricacy of
primitive cultures have often been a source of wonder to
wealthier, more modern people. The more sophisticated
non-Western cultures are endowed with ancient traditions,
distinctive graces, and powerful insights. Some have long
enjoyed levels of economic development which allowed
moderate prosperity to everyone and a heritage of high culture among an elite. Each has had its own golden ages of
prosperity and extraordinary achievement.

Third, culture and values should not be decided simply
on the basis of what works. I accept a modified form of
economic culture (Chapters 2 and 3), because it seems consistent with what I have come to believe about God from
revelation and experience. I think Christian values are, in
the long run, conducive to world development, but my
allegiance to them is derived from religious conviction, and
I do not count on any easy or obvious payoff. Thus, I ap-
plaud others who, because of different philosophic or religious convictions, reject the material attractions of modern
culture.

Fourth, as people get richer, it becomes less and less
clear that further economic growth would make them yet
happier or healthier, or further contribute to the causes of
beauty and truth. Ramgopal Agarwala, a colleague who
has been influential in a Friday-morning seminar of World
Bank staff interested in religious values and economic development, has been trying to convince us that many well-
off people are now experiencing negative returns on addi-
tional income. Taking off from a "basic needs" approach to
development for low-income countries, he suggests that

many people in richer countries have passed a "total needs" threshold—beyond which more food, more clothes, bigger houses, and more possessions may be desired, but do a person more harm than good. I am not sure how many people are so rich that they could not benefit from better services, like education for their children or nursing care in old age, but it is at least true that we experience diminishing returns on more and more income, if only because of the time constraint. People in the rich countries have become a "harried leisure class," rushing from work to house repair, to yoga classes and church meetings, to boating on the weekend, without enough time to fully enjoy anything.[5]

Finally, people who have inherited economic culture, already *richer*-than-thou, dare not pretend to be *holier*-than-thou. Nor can they be sure that their culture will guarantee continued affluence.

On this last point, it is instructive to compare those of us who enjoy the benefits of modern economic culture to ancient Israel. The beginnings of Christendom in decadent Rome and the Dark Ages were hardly more auspicious than the wanderings of early Israel. Yet Europeans were entrusted with the Word, and God's commands and promises shaped their history and culture. On the whole, the people who have inherited European culture have been unfaithful. The ostensibly religious Middle Ages were, in many ways, barbaric. Modern society is, to some extent, a conscious rebellion against God, and economic culture was spread throughout the world in a violent burst of arrogance and conquest.

The Old Testament prophets argued that God had blessed Israel for his name's sake, simply because he had revealed himself to them, despite their consistent disobedience. But Israel mistook his gifts for bounty from the amoral baals, spirits of agricultural and human fertility. Idolatry and immorality, according to the prophets, were to lead to

Israel's destruction. God could raise up other nations for his purposes.

The widespread modern presumption that blessings come automatically from their proximate causes—hard work, money, technology, or the like—is the equivalent of baal worship. God is patient, but when we work, consume, or manipulate technology without much attention to moral considerations, our idolatry invites curses.

We have seen how biblically derived ideals helped lead to the affluence of Europeans, the descendants of Europeans around the world, and the others who have made much of European culture their own. It is, however, as if God had blessed them for the sake of his Word among them, rather than for their faithfulness to it. The moral character of the people who have inherited modern culture is nothing anyone would want to imitate. It is, rather, the ideals which are extraordinary.

ECONOMIC CULTURE AND TRADITIONAL RELIGIONS

Economic culture is spreading throughout the world, and, particularly in developing countries, it is challenging and changing traditional religions. What people believe has a positive or negative impact on economic development.

Most architects of Third World development over the last generation, following the secular humanist tradition, have tended to relate to religions by attacking them all as superstitious, praising them all insofar as they teach common moral truths, or ignoring them and proceeding with the business of secular reform. But religion has too much influence on the development process to be ignored, and the differences among religions are significant and of practical importance for development.

Moreover, the tensions between religions and economic

culture may indicate inadequacies in economic culture. All the world's vital religions have absorbed much of economic culture's dynamism, a significant witness to its ethical reliability. But the world's religions are also unanimous in critiquing economic culture's horizontal, mechanical worldview, and each of the world's religions raises specific doubts about particular aspects of economic culture. Such questions of truth and ultimate purpose should be taken seriously as people reflect on the directions of their lives and of the world's development.

A lush variety of beliefs, practices, folklore, and customs are found within each religious tradition. But we can, without too much violence to the truth, analyze the religions which are vital in this century according to the following broad categories:

1. the Abrahamic family: Christianity, Judaism, and Islam; [6]
2. localized primal religions;
3. South Asian religion, including the many forms of Hinduism and Buddhism;
4. East Asian imperial religions: Confucianism and Shinto.

Economic culture is a secular child of the first group, the Abrahamic family of messianic faiths. It was born out of *Christianity*, bringing Christian ideals to fruition in everyday life. Yet economic culture was, in some respects, a rebellion against Christianity, and the church has been divided in its reactions. Some of the churches, at first mostly in the Protestant countries of northern Europe and North America, embraced humanist reform, perhaps too uncritically.

Other church leaders, however, mounted a holy alliance against modernity. Partly due to this conservative leadership, the majority of nominal Christians around the world are now behind the times. This includes many of the poor in Eastern Europe, Latin America, and the cultural backwoods of Western Europe and North America. With little ability to shape the future, they look to death or perhaps an army of angels to release them from this vale of tears. Unlettered, they approach God more often through prayer, feasts, and relics than through sermons or books. They tend to live by tradition, custom, and sacred rules. They are humble before both priests and bosses. Their world is clearly divided between "us" and "them," often along religious lines.

Part of the nominally Christian world has never been completely evangelized. In Latin America, for example, not more than 10% of the people are practicing Catholics.[7] Among the lower classes, Catholic devotion is sometimes almost lost in a welter of superstition and fatalism. Among intellectuals, unbelief is rife, often combined with resentment against the imposition of Catholicism as official doctrine among people who never internalized it.

In developed countries, too, some Christian groups are bastions of archaism and political conservatism. I am convinced that Christian faith should lead to "critical solidarity" with economic culture, but any empirical account of Christianity in North America would have to include conservative groups who find modernity less congenial to their faith than I do.

Judaism, like Christianity, has been divided in its reactions to economic culture. But reformers have had the upper hand in Judaism, primarily because of the importance of education in Jewish tradition. The Enlightenment was widely accepted among Jews, partly because it freed Jews from the ghettos to which they had been confined. Orthodox Jews remain somewhat other-worldly, tending toward abstract debate, legalism, and parochialism. But most Jews have abandoned detailed prescriptions of the law

and ethnic isolation, which are, by Enlightenment standards, unreasonable, illiberal, and sectarian. Most Jews
follow only enough of those traditions to maintain their
identity, concentrating on the universal ethical principles
of the law instead. Zionism, zeal for Israel's military defense and economic development, is a modern way of
maintaining Jewish peoplehood in an era at odds with the
more traditional distinguishing characteristics of Jewish
people.[8]

The other religion descended from Abraham, *Islam*, has
been the most solidly conservative of all the religions. It
shares biblical roots with Christians, Jews, and economic
culture. It is, in many ways, an apt religion for economic
development. Islam is even earthier than Christianity and
Judaism: the Prophet was a trader and a soldier, and Is-
lamic law is immediately applicable in business and military affairs. Islam is preeminently rational, too: Moslem
theology need not struggle with incarnation or sacraments,
and medieval Islam brought science and religion together
in a magnificent body of scholastic thought. Islam does not
separate Caesar's kingdom from God's, so the Moslem
world more quickly submitted its institutions to the
egalitarianism of divine law than did Europe. The ruling
class of the Ottoman Empire, for example, was exceptionally open to men of talent from any background.[9] The
vision of worldwide fraternity, which for Jews had remained
a dream, inspired Mohammed's armies to establish an empire which united the world from India to Spain.

The main conflict between Islam and economic culture
concerns the law. Seyyed Hossein Nasr, one of Islam's most
eloquent exponents, explained:

> Religion to a Muslim *is* essentially the Divine Law
> which includes not only universal moral principles
> but details how man should conduct his life and deal
> with his neighbor and with God; how he should eat,

procreate and sleep, how he should buy and sell at
the market place; how he should pray and perform
other acts of worship. It includes all aspects of human
life.[10]

Islam, like Judaism, gradually developed extremely detailed interpretations of the law. Although the principles
of Koranic law are humane, it has tended to be rigid and
static in its application. While Judaism has become more
liberal since the Enlightenment, the modern revival of
Islam has been almost entirely conservative. Many Moslems are liberal humanists, but there is virtually no Moslem
liberal humanism. That is, the elites of a number of Moslem countries are secularized and may disregard or seek
to reform Koranic traditions for the sake of economic development; but, even now, they have little Moslem religious
inspiration for social innovation.

Egypt and Turkey, the first Moslem states to modernize,
did so through secular revolution, partly directed against
Islam. Even Pakistan, which came into being for the sake
of Islam, has never been able to use Moslem law as a practical foundation for economic development. Population control programs in Egypt, Pakistan, India, and Bangladesh—all
places where they are urgently needed—have been hobbled
by objections based on Koranic law. The dominant trend in
Islam, led by the Wahhabiyah movement in Saudi Arabia
and strengthened by their oil wealth, is conservative. The
revolution in Iran, theologically and culturally conservative
but radical in its demands for social justice and demilitariza-
tion, might lead part of the Moslem world in a new direction if it proves viable. To date, however, the uncompromising fanaticism of the Iranian revolution has made stable
government and development difficult.

Those Moslems who believe that economic development
is a blessing from Allah which Islam should encourage
must, I think, eventually replace outmoded legalism with

something like the Christian ethic of creative love. Legalistic rigidity still hinders the Moslem world from fully taking part in the movement toward modernity which in so many ways expresses Moslem ideals.[11]

The three Abrahamic religions—Christianity, Judaism, and Islam—are all relatively young upstarts among the traditional religions. *Primal religion,* the second of the four categories, is much older. Within the category of primal religion, I include most of the traditional religions of Africa and of tribal and relatively isolated peoples elsewhere. These religions are many and diverse, but there are broad commonalities too: localized gods and beliefs, binding and slowly changing customs carried by oral tradition, and the struggle for survival as a prominent religious theme (appealing to the gods for fertile crops and for more children). The transition between primal religion and economic development is more of a crisis than Christians, Jews, and Moslems have had to face.

All the world religions and modern culture, too, have challenged primal religion. But most people, especially poor people, persist in attitudes which are characteristic of primal religion, regardless of whatever world-shaking message missionaries may have at some time convinced them to call their own. The average Buddhist in Thailand prays to the Lord Buddha and local spirits for material aid in this life and some sort of heaven in the next, and the average Christian in Latin America may approach Christ and his saints as manipulatively as a traditional African appealing to spirits in a local river. The persistent vitality of the occult and spiritism among otherwise secular Europeans and North Americans is only one more example of the tenacity of primal religion.

The primal worldview remains attractive because it is in accord with natural human longings and actual, firsthand experience of the world. The religious quest for this-worldly blessing—for prosperity, fertility, healing, success—is as natural as a child crying for help in the night. No matter how we try to broaden our perspective, our understanding is still parochial. Primal religion makes no pretense to universality: its ethics relate to family and tribe; its claims to truth are partial; and its devotion is focused on a few among admittedly many gods.[12]

Economic culture contradicts primal religion almost point for point. The two agree in purpose: prosperity and success. But they could hardly be more at odds with regard to means. Primal religion tends to appeal to the elders' wisdom, and inherited knowledge and institutions are considered sacred. Local traditions, which tightly knit traditional communities together, tend not to encourage creativity, and they sometimes frustrate efforts toward national and international unity. Status is assigned by custom, not achievement.

When two cultures clash, the technologically superior culture usually replaces the other by a process of threat and intimidation. In this case, the richer nations easily conquered primitive peoples. Now national elites have everywhere replaced colonial officials, but they share in modern culture and the prosperity it brings. Almost everywhere, primal religion is on the retreat.

The *Hinduism* and *Buddhism* of the masses in South Asia have much in common with primal religion, but the high traditions of these religions are quite different. While the primal religious urge is to recruit the spirits for aid in this life, South Asian religion, more sophisticated, offers ways of overcoming and ultimately escaping from mundane life.

The final goal of life, in classic Hindu philosophy, is for the soul to realize its unity with Brahman, the impersonal Oneness underlying all appearances. The world as we nor-

mally experience it is *maya,* that is confusion and deception.
One can make spiritual progress through successive rein-
carnations by ritual observance, fulfilling caste duties, good
works, or asceticism. The ultimate goal, however, is mystic
unity. Ethical considerations are secondary; even Radhar-
krishnan, always at pains to emphasize the ethical aspect
of Hinduism, admits:

> While the sacred scriptures of the Hebrews and the
> Christians are more religious and ethical, those of the
> Hindus are more spiritual and contemplative. The
> one fact of life in India is the Eternal Being of God.[13]

The primary means to realization of this "one fact of life"
is mystic detachment:

> Thinking about sense-objects
> Will attach you to sense-objects;
> Grow attached and you become addicted;
> Thwart your addiction, it turns to anger.[14]

The inner connection between desire and suffering, already explained in this passage from the *Bhagavad-Gita,*
was the basis for the Buddha's more radical detachment
from normal life. The Buddha taught that

> birth is suffering, old age is suffering, death is suffer-
> ing, to be united with what one loves is suffering, to
> be separated from what one loves is suffering, not to
> attain one's desire is suffering.[15]

Desire attached to the transient objects of this life is bound
to result in suffering, so the only cure for suffering is to
overcome desire. In order to overcome desire, the Buddha
recommended the Noble Path of moderate living, compassion, and meditation.

The ultimate goal is *nirvana,* the blessed peace of enlightened detachment from desire. One scripture (the
Dhammapada) describes nirvana thus:

When the wise man by earnestness hath driven
Vanity far away, the terraced heights
Of wisdom doth he climb, and, free from care,
Looks down on the vain world, the careworn crowd—
As he who stands upon a mountaintop
Can watch, serene himself, the toilers on the plains.[16]

Buddhism's original other-worldliness was tempered somewhat as it grew from a monastic movement into the religion of entire nations. Buddhist monks assumed a place within the social order, providing ritual services and education to the people and lending religious purpose and legitimacy to kings. In the Mahayana traditions which developed in China and Japan, the Buddha's stern philosophy to some extent gave way to tantrism, Zen, the worship of *bodhisatt-vas,* and other innovations. Some Mahayana sects came to stress concern for this world, family obligations, and civic responsibility, so it would be wrong to say that traditional Buddhism has always preached against involvement in this world, even though that is an important aspect of its original and dominant message.

Although many Hindus and Buddhists fully enjoy the good things of this world and work for material progress, the general direction of both religions is fundamentally away from the desires and confusions of this world. Although both religions cultivate a passion for truth, modern science and technology were foreign to South Asia before Europe's influence, partly because Hinduism and Buddhism lacked the doctrine of creation; there was less reason to expect the marvelous consistency which makes nature amenable to rational description. It has been argued that there was less motive for technological improvement, since worldly pursuits often did not enjoy enthusiastic religious sanction.

Regarding liberty, equality, and fraternity, the impulses of Hinduism and Buddhism are mixed. The caste system, long accepted within Hinduism but rejected by the Buddha, is the opposite of liberty and equality. Both religions, however, teach human fraternity. Buddhism focuses on the common predicament of mankind and, as a missionary religion, has united a large part of Asia in devotion to the Buddha. Hinduism, on the other hand, assumes that everyone is already one with Brahman, whether they know it or not. It is catholic and supple, allowing each culture, each caste, each time of life its distinctive spirit, assuming that the countless gods to which people bow are only his million faces. Its unity is syncretistic rather than missionary, absorbing the best insights of the movements which have challenged it.

Both Hinduism and Buddhism have experienced considerable reform and revival during the last century. While primal religions have tended to lose credibility quickly when confronted with the wider world, and Islam has generally fought against foreign influence, both Hinduism and Buddhism, flexible and highly reflective, have, to some extent, absorbed economic culture into themselves.

The tradition of Hindu syncretism has allowed it to grow relatively painlessly, combining its own mysticism with a Christian ethic of love and humanist hope for the world. The pioneers of this change were nineteenth century teachers like Ram Mohun Roy and Ramakrishna, who found their inspiration in both traditional and Western sources. Modern Hindu teachers have tended to be critical of the way the caste system usually functions in India and of much of the rest of popular religious practice. They have instead defended Hinduism primarily on the basis of its ancient, rational, and inclusive philosophy. Mahatma Gandhi, more than anyone else, symbolizes the new Hinduism—open to modernity, reformist, and political, yet embodying traditional Hindu wisdom and virtue.[17]

Buddhism, too, had its nineteenth century reformers, like

Prince Monjkut of Siam. And, as in Hinduism, the modern revival of Buddhism gathered intensity and popularity from the nationalist movement of this century. In almost every country, Buddhism has become more rational, this-worldly, and political:

• *Rational.* A recurring theme among the modern defenders of Buddhism has been the rationality of the Buddha's original teaching. Buddhism is empirical, more like science than faith. This theme has implied a critique of less rational folkways, a return to the original Buddhist scriptures, a resurgence of interest in meditation, and the improvement of monastic education.

• *This-worldly.* Modernizing Buddhists have rejected the stereotype of Buddhism as an other-worldly, pessimistic religion. In the process, lay Buddhists have claimed a more active religious role, Buddhist hospitals and relief centers have been established, and monastic education and teaching have been modernized. Several programs link Buddhism directly to economic development, the most successful of them a village revitalization movement in Sri Lanka (Sarvodaya) which gives equal emphasis to spiritual renewal and material improvements.

• *Political.* In a number of countries, Buddhism's new relevance to this-worldly society has extended into politics. In Thailand, undisrupted by colonialism, Buddhist monks continue in their traditionally conservative role of support for the king and his government. But in several other countries, where colonialism threatened Buddhism's hegemony, Buddhism developed into a more activist, dissident political force. And in Japan one Buddhist sect, Soka Gokkai, has also become an important political party.[18]

If Hinduism and Buddhism have retained their identity while, to some extent, changing their content, the two great East Asian imperial religions, *Confucianism* and *Shinto*, have nearly lost their identity, but their ancient traditions continue to be influential. Both have been suppressed since the Second World War, but the behavior of most Chinese, Japanese, and Koreans is still steeped in these religious traditions.

Confucianism and Shinto were the least other-worldly of the great religions. The high traditions of both concentrated on good government and this-worldly happiness. They were little concerned with cosmological speculation. When Confucius was asked about worshiping spirits and about death, he replied, "We don't know yet about life, how can we know about death? We don't know yet how to serve men, how can we know about serving spirits?" [19]

As Europe first came into contact with China, China was superior in almost every respect: better government, less war, finer culture and manners, more advanced technology. Europe was changing quickly, but in 1793, when England sent its first diplomatic mission to Peking, China's emperor's self-assurance was justifiable. He wrote to George III:

> You, O King, live beyond the confines of many seas; nevertheless, impelled by your humble desire to partake of the benefits of our civilization you have dispatched a mission respectfully bearing your memorial. . . . The earnest terms in which it is cast reveal a respectful humility on your part, which is highly praiseworthy. If you assert that your reverence for our Celestial Dynasty fills you with a desire to acquire our civilization, our ceremonies and code of law differ so completely from your own that, even if your Envoy were able to acquire the rudiments of our civilization, you could not possibly transplant our manners and customs to your alien soil. Therefore, however adept the Envoy might become, nothing would be gained thereby.[20]

If China's tea, silk, and procelain were absolute necessities for the English, the emperor was willing to let them continue buying at Canton. With respect to England's desire for regular trade, however, the Emperor wrote:

> Swaying the wide world, I have but one aim in view, namely, to maintain a perfect governance and to fulfill the duties of the state: strange and costly objects do not interest me. I . . . have no use for your country's manufactures. . . . Our Celestial Empire possesses all things in prolific abundance and lacks no product within its borders. There is therefore no need to import the manufactures of outside barbarians in exchange for our own produce.

Such confidence may have kept China from modernizing in time to defend itself against the aggression of the more modern nations of Europe, Russia, the United States, and Japan. Chinese culture had always been hierarchical and authoritarian, and by the nineteenth century it had become rigid and reactionary, too.

Even when China undertook its program of revolutionary modernization under Mao Tse-tung, it remained authoritarian. Modern values were imposed from above. As a student at the London School of Economics in 1974-75, I became acquainted with half a dozen students from the People's Republic of China. They were impressive individuals, selected for their intelligence and exemplary virtue, but what impressed me most was their intellectual solidarity. Whenever we discussed issues in the school coffee shop, we Westerners would debate among ourselves as much as with the Chinese, but they would always take the party line. It is only recently that the inclinations toward individual liberty which flowered in republican China, before Communism, have been allowed expression again.

Japan modernized much earlier than China. Some of Japan's traditional leaders decided to adopt enough Western culture to maintain independence. Japan's modernization was perhaps even more authoritarian than that of China, certainly more militaristic. Japan had remained feudalistic and militaristic under a veneer of Confucianism borrowed from China. Japan's modernization was accomplished on command of the hierarchy for military reasons. Ancient Shinto was transformed into a nationalist, imperial, modernizing religion. Only after defeat in the Second World War did Japan embark on a more peaceful, liberal development path.

Japan remains very much Japan, having folded the dynamism, technology, and political liberalism of the West into its own cultural tradition. The mix has been an economic wonder, the best example yet of the possibilities of accepting key elements of economic culture without wholesale adoption of any ideology or religion from the West.

CULTURE CHANGE AND CHRISTIAN MISSION

The values of economic culture are logically and intrinsically related to economic development. The initial "take-off" of Protestant countries like Holland and England, which inspired Weber's *The Protestant Ethic and the Spirit of Capitalism,* has been followed by take-offs throughout Europe and among European peoples in North America and Oceania, in the U.S.S.R. and Japan, and more recently in the Koreas, Iran, Mexico, Brazil, and China. Dozens of other countries around the globe have started to rise economically, perhaps not "taking off" like a rocket, but still enjoying a steady increase in prosperity. There are now many proven cultural paths to development. Growth has been associated with most of the same economic values everywhere, but they have often been thoroughly detached from their Christian origins.

Economic culture has been conveyed around the world primarily by secular forces like capitalism, foreign influence, Communism, and nationalism:

• Capitalism invites change by offering choice. Through radio ads, provocative signboards, and new goods in local shops, it woos people to work and save their way into the strange new world of bourgeois satisfaction. Through industrial labor, it schools the traditional poor in bourgeois discipline and the possibilities of upward mobility. The way capitalistic development changes culture is vividly documented in Lisa Peattie's anthropological study of a poor *barrio* in Venezuela.[21]

• During the colonial era the imperial European states imposed "civilization" on the poor. The influence of the rich and powerful countries continues, but now usually only at the permission of independent governments in developing countries. Third World students flock to universities in the rich countries. Books and movies, business people and tourists, aid and ideas flow into developing countries from the richer countries. These are all, in various ways, bearers of economic culture.

• Communism is the fundamentalism of economic culture—explaining everything in terms of material relationships, justifying anything in the name of progress, and claiming scientific truth as the only truth. Individual freedom is Communism's avowed final goal, but for now equality and fraternity are pursued with a vengeance. Communism has taken on many of the characteristics of a traditional religion: a revered founder and sacred scriptures, saints and martyrs, doctrinal disputes, ceremonies and festivals. Communist dogma has been imposed on more than a third of mankind as official, state religion. Any forced conversion generates more conformity than zeal, and there are probably fewer devout Marxists in Eastern Europe than in Western Europe. In the developing countries where Communism has been imposed, however, modern values have been more successfully inculcated through revivalistic political campaigns.

• Nationalism can also be used to motivate modern attitudes. Attempts to fabricate nationalistic modernizing religions (Nkrumah's pseudo-religious symbolism in Ghana, for example) have soon cracked and been forgotten.[22] But a number of Third World leaders (Nyerere in Tanzania, for example) continue to exhort their people to practice economic virtues out of patriotism. In countries where nearly everyone has the same religious background, political leaders can harness religion and nationalism together in the service of development. Virtually everywhere at least political speeches and school civics lessons urge people to work hard for development for the nation's sake. In Third World countries where nationalism runs strong, it has been a powerful force for cultural change.

The trouble with all four of these modernizing forces—capitalism, neocolonialism, Communism, and nationalism—is that they are so *thoroughly* modern. They are narrowly focused on this-worldly progress. They seldom inspire queries about the adequacy or depth of modern values, and they have nothing to say about abiding concerns like death and guilt, which predate modernity. They tend to be one-sided—totalitarian or individualistic, dependent or adamantly independent. As patently human creations, they cannot endow people's lives with transcendent dignity and meaning, and ought not elicit total loyalty.

The broader resources of humanism—art, history, and philosophy—can offer some historic and critical perspective on narrowly economic culture. The reform movements within the traditional religions also offer more depth. Even while religions struggle to adapt themselves to modern aspirations, they continue to question and transcend modernity. Nearly all of them continue to insist that there is some tension between God and the world, between ultimate reality and contemporary illusion.

Christianity, always both the agent and the critic of modern values, is increasingly influential in the developing countries. The balance within Christianity is shifting toward the Third World. Almost limited to Europe from the seventh to nineteenth centuries, Christianity has finally become a worldwide religion. The church has lost some of its vitality and appeal in the countries where the gospel tented for so many centuries, while it is growing quickly elsewhere, particularly in Africa and Indonesia. If present trends continue, most of the Christians in the world in the year 2000 will *not* be white.[23] Will the gospel assist the Third World peoples who are accepting it in their economic development? Or was the association of biblical faith, in particular Reformation Christianity, with prosperity among Europeans a unique historical coincidence?

The values which Christians believe to be at the heart of the universe are also at the heart of the world's economic development. These values are spreading in cultural movements divorced from faith, but perhaps biblical materialism —holy, humble, and free—is the style of development most worthy of human aspiration. It is certainly less offensive than either totalitarian coercion or individualistic greed, and more transcendent than either colonial imposition or nationalistic fervor. If the thinking in Chapters 3 and 4 is right, biblical materialism also tends to be more satisfying, balanced, and sustainable than secular versions of economic culture.

Christian evangelists have seldom focused primarily on economic development, but many have been aware of the relationship between faith and development. The diary of J. Rebbman, for example, the first white man to trek to Mount Kilimanjaro (in 1849) noted how, having shown an African king a blanket, candle, and umbrella

> I took my Bible in my hand, and said, that it was to
> that book that we Europeans owed the things he had
> just seen. . . . Our forefathers had lived in the same
> ignorance as themselves, until they had received the
> Word of God as contained in the book.[24]

Rebbman simplistically believed that evangelism was the
long-term basis for development.

M. M. Thomas, a twentieth century Indian theologian,
analyzed the historic impact of Christian mission on development more precisely:

> If today the people of India are committed to strive
> for a new society . . . it is due, in part at least, to
> the transformation of traditional spirituality made
> possible by the impact of the gospel of Christ, not
> only as presented by Christian missions but also as
> mediated, first through western culture and later
> through the Indian cultural renaissance. Of course,
> even in the Christian mission, not to speak of the
> movements and attitudes it promoted, the gospel was
> often present in distorted forms and in association
> with many western idols, and it is difficult to say
> which made the greater spiritual impact on Indian
> spirituality—the gospel of Christ or the western idols.
> But no historian will deny that the gospel did play
> a decisive role. That is to say, the spiritual creativity
> behind today's revolutionary search for a society
> which harnesses nature through science and tech-
> nology for human welfare, eliminates poverty and
> oppression, and opens the door of participation in
> power structures to hitherto submerged groups, and
> moves toward a fraternity of free and equal persons
> has its source, in part at least, in Christ's salvation
> of the human spirit.[25]

On all three continents of the Third World, conversion
to Christianity has benefited the whole man, not only the
soul. Many contemporary African leaders acknowledge that
the Christian mission in Africa gave them the education

they needed to eventually overcome colonial domination and lead their nations into modern prosperity. The Asian church was recruited mostly from tribal peoples and scheduled castes, yet its members are generally prospering and have an admirable record of service to their nations. Similarly, as Pentecostalism and the "basic community" movement intensify the faith of nominal Catholics in Latin America, the results in terms of personal reform and political awareness have been dramatic.[26]

The mission situation is now drastically different from what it was during the colonial era, of course. The pretensions of the white-skinned, traditionally Christian nations have been humbled, and the world has gained new respect for Third World peoples and cultures.

Christian mission is no longer a matter of sending missionaries from Europe and North America to the Third World. The gospel has been planted nearly everywhere, and local church leaders are much more influential than foreigners. Ecumenical sharing—from Asia to South America, from Africa to North America, from South America to Europe, as well as in the more traditional directions—has replaced paternalistic mission.

The valid experiences and insights of other religious traditions are being taken more seriously within Christian life and thought. Distinctively Asian theologies, like that of Kosuke Kayama, are being articulated within the church.[27] Latin American theology seems to have gained its own voice through identification with the struggles of the poor for liberation from local and foreign oppression. And Christianity has taken root in African culture, too, most dramatically Africanized through the emergence of thousands of indigenous churches. My first book, *Eden Revival* (Concordia, 1975) was a study of some of these churches in which Africans worship Christ with dancing and drumming, faith healing, visions, and trance experience.

The contemporary evangelist begins with faith that Jesus is Lord and Savior of all, but needs to be open to what is valuable in the aspirations, both traditional and modern, of non-Christians. Why? First, an awareness of our own limitations makes such openness the only honest stance. Second, we Christians believe God has made all peoples in his image, that he has been active in the whole world's history, and that he cherishes each individual identity. Third, many people's sense of identity has been shaken or insulted by the spread of economic culture.

Ivan Illich expressed the outrage the poor must sometimes feel as traditional values are attacked:

> I submit that foreign gods (ideals, idols, ideologies, persuasions, values) are more offensive to the "poor" than the military and economic power of the foreigner. It is more irritating to feel seduced to the consumption of overpriced sugar-water called Coca-Cola than to submit helplessly to doing the same job an American does, only at half the pay. It angers a person more to hear a priest preach cleanliness, thrift, resistance to socialism, or obedience to unjust authority, than to accept military rule. . . . There is no exit from a way of life built on $5,000-plus per year, and there is no possible road leading into this way of life for nine out of ten men in our generation and the next. And for the nine it is revolting to hear a message of economic and social salvation presented by the affluent that, however sincerely expressed, leads the "poor" to believe that it is their fault that they do not fit into God's world as it should be and as it has been decreed that it should be around the North Atlantic.[28]

The poor are really poor, however, not, as in the passage above, "poor." And although they will not be radically better off for generations, they must adopt some values more prevalent among the affluent if they want to be much better off at all. That too, although galling, is true. They can do without Coca-Cola, and, if Illich has his way, even without schools, but they probably cannot be healthy without cleanliness, secure without thrift, or literate without education.

Economic culture is not gospel. It is, in the main, a righteous cultural movement, but it does not come as good news. It makes demands on both rich and poor. It calls for revolutionary change in the life-style and politics of both rich and poor.

Why did Jesus call the poor blessed? Because they do not need to reform themselves? On the contrary, it is relatively obvious to the poor, despite Illich's protest, that they do not fit into God's world as it should be. It is also acutely obvious to the poor that the rich, more willing to advise than to share, do not fit into God's world as it should be either. As John Richard Neuhaus wrote in a review of liberation theology:

> The poor are redemptive in the sense that the whole society discovers the truth about itself along its fault lines, at the points of its weaknesses rather than at the points of its greatest strength.[29]

The poor are called blessed because of the promise of the Kingdom, and many of the poor may be especially receptive to transcendent promises, because they cannot help but be aware of the evils within and around them.

The call to repentance must remain part of the Christian message, also among the poor. The conversion required is never to an alien culture, however, but to the purposes for which God intended each people. And the more important part of the Christian message is not ethics at all, but the gospel: through Jesus Christ we are loved by God, even if we have been rich and greedy, or poor and lazy. It may be that only God's forgiving presence is gentle enough to evoke radical change voluntarily and without loss of face.

7

The Spiritual Core

By way of summary, it might be worthwhile to piece together from various chapters what *holy materialism* might look like in a nation, a church, or an individual.

At the level of the nation, we can reiterate several economic policy recommendations that have been developed from Christian values in earlier chapters of this book:

1. a steady course of macroeconomic management, without demands for either full employment or stable prices immediately;

2. full realization of energy and resources scarcity, appropriate price increases, and public measures to develop alternatives to petroleum and other scarce resources;

3. attention to traditional concerns of the Left: poverty; racism and sexism; inadequate public services; overly optimistic, technological health care; and abuses of private power and wealth.

We can also mention again the sort of orientation toward the developing countries which, it seems to me, a Christian understanding of economic values suggests:

1. dismantling of the last vestiges of colonialism and flexibility toward Third World nationalism;

2. negotiations toward a New International Economic Order;

3. continued pressure on our government and Third World governments for the sake of basic human needs (like food) and basic human rights.

In thinking about a model congregation or denomination, one would expect, first of all, that it be an advocate of people who are down and out. If a congregation wants to bring its faith to bear on economic life, it should be involved with troubled people in its own area. It should also provide some leadership to denominational and ecumenical programs of involvement in social issues. There should be a steady flow of prayers, money, and political support (lobbying, voting, campaigning) to people in need far away. Study-action groups, at both local and national levels, might specialize on particular political issues.

One would expect a model church's members to be helping each other live out economic values in their moderated, Christian forms. Families might be invited together to think and pray about their life-styles. Children's religious educa-tion would include exposure to economic and social issues, and the church's young people would probably be choosing careers that would place them on the frontiers of society's development.

And if we were to find an exemplar individual, what would he or she be like? We would expect such a person to possess and consume less than normal, and perhaps work less too, but to heartily enjoy good food, works of art, and other this-worldly goods. We would not be surprised to find him calmly engaged in a losing cause, or giving assistance in some nearly hopeless situation. He might well have made some unexpected changes in his life, maybe abandon-ing a successful career in midlife, for example, to do more worthwhile work. We would look for a sensible person. He should be active in politics, and as sensible about public affairs as about his own. We would expect him to be a pioneer in ecologically responsible ways of living.

This exemplar individual should be charitable—generous to people in need with his time, money, and political sentiments. His compassion and sense of justice should be evident in his dealings with family, friends, and community. But it should extend as well to people in need who live in other parts of the country or other parts of the world. We would be disappointed if he were not somehow involved in the problems of developing countries—perhaps hosting a foreign student, giving extra support to his denomination's work abroad, or following the foreign-aid bill through Congress.

Our model of holy materialism should surprise us somehow, too. He will be himself—creative, perhaps wrong, but free. When Arthur Simon, director of Bread for the World, read these pages in an earlier draft, he wrote back:

> The exemplar individual you describe is rare enough, that's for sure. But somehow he seems placid compared to the Sermon on the Mount, say, or some of the Old and New Testament models that we have: Jesus, John, Paul, Peter, Amos, or Jeremiah.

What's missing in the description so far? Surprise—the surprise of the Spirit in each one of God's people—the individuality, the adventure, the bold freedom.

Missing, too, is credibility, because no real person is a perfect model of virtue. St. Paul was a bit arrogant and cantankerous. St. Peter's quick temper was notorious. Amos would have been hard to get along with even if he had not been a prophet, and Jeremiah felt sorry for himself. There is no exemplar person, church, or nation—only struggling and forgiven ones.

Up to this point, this book has been mostly about Christian ethical values. What policies should the nation re-

consider? What should churches do? How should a person
live? But ethics are not the most important part of Christianity. The core of Christian experience is rather the grace
of God.

Values which were transmitted to the modern world primarily through Christianity are now accepted far beyond
the boundaries of the church. Many secular humanists,
drawing on wider resources in the arts and philosophy, and
reformers in other religious traditions too, approach the
values of economic culture with nearly the same reserva-
tions and realism which for me are based on a Christian
critique. But not many people outside the Christian faith
share in Christianity's emphasis on God's mercy and forgiveness. It is the most distinctive aspect of Christian life.
Does God's grace have any relevance to economics?

The rest of this chapter reviews the revelation of God's
grace, discusses the impracticality of simply imitating divine
grace in economic affairs, and then describes how grace can,
nevertheless, be the inner core of a holy materialism.

GOD'S GRACE TOWARD SINNERS

Already in the Old Testament the Lord was depicted
in agony, struggling with himself over what to do with sin
and evil in the world. Justice and mercy wrestled within
him; again and again he was more merciful than his own
law would warrant. He picked the nation of Israel for no
good reason, prospered them even though they consistently
disobeyed the law, and promised luxurious future blessings
even as he prepared to punish their sins. The prophets compared the Lord to a foolish husband, repeatedly cuckolded
by a promiscuous wife. The prophet Hosea married a whore
to dramatize God's long-suffering patience with Israel. Even
when the Lord's pent-up wrath broke out on Israel, he could
not bear to destroy them completely:

> My heart recoils within me,
> my compassion grows warm and tender. . . .
> for I am God and not man,
> the Holy One in your midst,
> and I will not come to destroy (Hosea 11:8-9).

In his dealings with Israel the Lord expressed the compassion he had enjoined on them with respect to their neighbors in need. People consistently fall short of imitating him; it is scandalous, not that relatively righteous people sometimes suffer, but that wicked people continue to prosper so long.

God has a special affection for the nation to which he revealed himself first, but he could hardly bear to destroy other nations for their sins either. The prophet Jonah was sent to Nineveh in Assyria, the arch-enemy of Israel, a contemporary symbol of corruption. When Nineveh repented in response to his word of judgment from the Lord, Jonah went into the wilderness and pouted. He was upset that his prophecy of doom would not come true. But the Lord refused to destroy even Nineveh, because he cared for all the men, women, children, and cattle in the city.

The Lord's long-suffering patience with sinners climaxed in the life and death of Jesus Christ. He was God among us, the Lord of life, able to give all the blessings the Old Testament Scriptures teach us to expect from God. He made no one rich, but he healed the sick, exorcised demons, fed the hungry, and raised the dead. He forgave sinners, associating with prostitutes and with tax collectors who had sold out to the hated Romans.

He taught radical trust and sharing:

> Is not life more than food, and the body more than clothing? . . . Why are you anxious about clothing? Consider the lilies of the field, how they grow; they neither toil nor spin; yet I tell you, even Solomon in all his glory was not arrayed like one of these (Matt. 6:25, 28).

> If anyone would sue you and take your coat, let him
> have your cloak as well; and if any forces you to go
> one mile, go with him two miles (Matt. 5:40-41).

Our violent world—devoted to getting and spending,
rather than trusting and sharing—engulfed and consumed
Jesus. The Gospels report how incredulous the disciples
were when Jesus began to teach "that the Son of Man
must suffer many things, and be rejected by the elders and
the chief priests and the scribes, and be killed, and after
three days rise again" (Mark 8:31). The disciples hid when
Jesus was arrested; his death had crushed their original
expectations for the Kingdom.

It was only after his resurrection that they came to understand his death as the final expression of God's unwill-
ingness to give sinners—even cowardly disciples—their due.
The cross, initially a bewilderment, came to be understood
as the climax of God's forbearance.

The disciples then went out into all the world preaching
about the grace God had shown in the life, death, and
resurrection of Jesus. The Word of God's grace has been
passed from disciple to disciple, from person to person,
from generation to generation since then. It is carried by
the church, the community of believers, in its preaching
and sacraments and mutual encouragement.

Because Jesus Christ was the Son of God, he could take
on himself the sin of the world. His death demonstrated the
deadly seriousness of God's judgment against sin. At the
same time, his forgiving submission to his first-century
enemies was the incarnation of God's suffering patience
with sinners of all time. Jesus' resurrection signaled that
his life and death were of cosmic significance.

For Jesus' sake, God blesses sinners. This includes mundane blessings, but he also blesses sinners by restoring their
relationship with himself. Peace with God is unspeakably
more important than any economic concerns, but it touches

the root problem of mammon worship. The gospel of grace through Christ is the power and the glory, without which Christian ethics would be a bed of nails.

GRACE VERSUS ECONOMICS

Divine grace contradicts the normal experience of the world. Life and society have hard edges. If you study, you get good marks. If you work, you get paid. We live in a world of limits, laws, and tough choices. God's grace does not excuse us from tough choices in this world, and choices are precisely what economics is about. Eugene Nida, for many years executive secretary of the American Bible Society, once remarked that the Christian's experience of grace is the opposite of economics. God's grace is virtually limitless; only our desire for it is limited. But in most situations economists are right to assume that virtually unlimited human desire has to choose among limited goods.[1]

Ordering economic affairs requires tough-mindedness. That is obvious in family budgeting. It is also true of national economic management: there is a trade-off, for example, between inflation and unemployment. We cannot, it seems, reduce inflation without making it harder for people to find jobs or move from job to job. If we are to return to stable prices and prosperity, there are tough decisions to be made and maintained: to tolerate some unemployment and some inflation. If voters pretend to themselves that the economy is soft and gracious, and demand easy solutions to economic problems from their representatives, their error will become obvious as economic conditions deteriorate even further.

In my work at the World Bank on projects designed to serve the urban poor, I continually find myself recommending tougher policies toward the poor. Apparently merciful policies are often unrealistic and, in the end, harmful to the poor. In many Third World cities, for example, well-meaning politicians have promised cheap or free water to the poor. But that may mean that the municipal water company soon runs out of funds, so that large areas of the city will never be reached by water pipes at all. In many Latin American cities, poor people have ended up paying 10 to 25 times as much per liter for unsanitary water delivered in tanker trucks than do people in richer parts of town who have enough political influence to get pipes laid in their neighborhoods. Our projects help finance water pipes for the poor, but normally only on the condition that the water company starts charging people for the water they get, or that any program of subsidies can be sustained to cover the growing population of the urban poor.[2]

I was once looking for an appropriate Bible passage to post on my office wall in the Urban Projects Department. I thought of Revelation 21, about the heavenly Jerusalem. What did I find in St. John's vision of God's future? It will be like a city—complex and somehow including human accomplishments—not another Garden of Eden. But as I searched for an apt quotation, I was surprised to learn that the things St. John praised in his vision of the New Jerusalem would disqualify it as a World Bank urban project:

"I will give from the fountain of the water of life without payment."	Unrealistic financial system.
"The street of the city was pure gold. . . ."	We insist on affordable standards.
"But nothing unclean shall enter it. . . ."	Legislating against garbage is not enough to solve the urban garbage problem.
"It had a great high wall with twelve gates. . . ."	Monumental architecture.
"The wall was built of jasper."	Inappropriate building technology.

St. John knew first-hand the filth and squalor of first century cities, and he envisioned a city with all those problems fantastically reversed. It was an image of this physical world eventually transformed into a gracious world, an image which is particularly striking to someone who is involved in the stingy details of trying to make the cities of this world serve the poor just a little more adequately.

I still concur in the Bank's insistence on tough-minded approaches to the problems of mass poverty. The New Jerusalem has yet to arrive. I went to work the next day, not with a quotable phrase to guide my work, but with a renewed vision of what God will someday do with the city of man and a new consciousness of how far removed from ordinary experience is his grace.

THE SECRET FEAST

What, then, does grace have to do with economics?

First, it is our relationship to God, established on the basis of his grace, which gives economic values, in their tempered and moderate Christian forms, legitimacy and motive power. Our Father created the world, so we in his image continue his creative work with the things of this world. He is dynamic, so we look forward to change. He is rational, so we expect regularity in the world. He is absolutely free, and has created us to share in his liberty. He shows no partiality, so we believe everyone is essentially equal. He is one Father, so we consider all humanity to be our family. The inner consistency of these six values is his personality.

God, who has revealed himself fully in Christ Jesus, is the goal toward which the world strains, also in this age of materialism. It is no surprise to believers that God's blessing follows the realization of these values even among people who do not fully know him, or that many unbelievers have learned their practicality from experience. Yet it is difficult to imagine any firm basis for this morality other than faith that they are grounded in the Absolute. A knowledge of his Word imparts a clearer direction to our groping, helps in identifying the heresies of the age, and sustains our efforts toward world development in his image.

The personal relationship we enjoy with God evokes in us the imitation of his character. Just as a husband and wife learn to share each other's dreams and, in time, become more like one another than they were on their wedding day, association with the almighty Lover through Word, sacraments, and Christian fellowship gently remolds the believer. Hope, a passion for truth, and a biblical sense of justice gradually become structures of our own character. The experience of God's sacrificial love for us in Jesus Christ germinates some imitation of divine love for all people in the believer. Fear can enforce "Thou shalt not," but only divine companionship can motivate a free and restless search for unexplored paths of righteousness.

Second, God's grace in Jesus Christ provides inner refreshment for Christian ethics. The judgments of the marketplace—how much we earn, or the car we can afford —pressure us. The ideals of economic culture judge us too: when we fail to progress; when we lose control of ourselves and act irrationally; or when we give preferential treatment, as we often do, to certain people because of superior intelligence, professional status, or wealth. Distinctively Christian morality is no escape from judgment. On the contrary, who can read the Sermon on the Mount, with its injunctions to carefree, selfless love, without feeling spiritually inadequate?

The forgiveness of God is a sabbath, a rest we can enjoy even while we struggle to buy a car, or love a neighbor. Forgiveness gives us opportunity, day after day and hour after hour, to begin again. It gives us the mystic bliss of unity with God, even while we fail and flounder morally.

The grace of God is the secret of people like Padre Garcia, a man I met one holiday morning in Guayaquil, Ecuador. Virtually the entire city was closed, but Padre Garcia's factory was open. He and several workers make prefab wood-and-cane houses which cost about $300 each. They have been in operation now about five years, providing affordable shelter to the poor. Padre Garcia's little houses dot the low-income areas of the city, including illegal settlements. What impressed me most about him was not his tireless work or accomplishments, but his irrepressible joy. He has every reason to be tired or cynical. He is an old man in a torn T-shirt; he works almost alone, and the people he serves are neglected by most of the institutions of society. But Padre Garcia almost giggles with delight in meeting a stranger, in telling about his factory, climbing over lumber and machinery—in living.

Third, God's grace is the promise of things to come. In the New Jerusalem there will be unlimited abundance—streets paved with gold, feasting for all, no more tears. There will be an abundance of knowledge of the Lord. No longer will anyone need to be reminded to obey God; we will all know and conform spontaneously to his will.

Now we see him as if through dark glass, but then we will see him face to face. Now we know in part, but then completely.

Fourth, grace transcends economic concerns. Economic development can help us overcome nature's inertia, but does not even hint at where we should be going. Economic development without the full Word can provide better husks to prodigal man, but only divine grace can welcome him home to the Father.[3] Economic development can make life better, but does not give us any hope beyond death.

Our Friday-morning World Bank discussion group on religious values and economic development includes a Danish humanist, who concluded his presentation one Friday with words such as these:

> I've been asked to talk about fundamental values and development on the basis of the Scandinavian experience. It frightens me, actually. The Scandinavian countries are examples of what many other countries would like to be. They have no poverty; Scandinavians enjoy high incomes and full security; they suffer no serious social conflicts. Yet the result? Many Scandinavians are bored.

I do not quote my Danish colleague here to derogate the social advances of Scandinavia or to comfort the readers of this "letter back home" about the social problems we have in the United States, but rather as a reminder that people need something beyond all the imaginations of economic culture.

Divine grace can make economic life eucharistic. We give thanks before each ordinary meal, as we give thanks at Holy Communion, that God is in our bread and wine. He is present. He is with us. And it is his persistent presence in the world which can give us hope for it and a sense of holy joy in material things.

> *Let the vineyards be fruitful, Lord,*
>   *and fill to the brim our cup of blessing;*
> *gather a harvest from the seeds that were sown,*
>   *that we may be fed with the bread of life.*
> *Gather the hopes and dreams of all,*
>   *unite them with the prayers we offer;*
> *grace our table with your presence,*
>   *and give us a foretaste of the feast to come.*[4]

Notes

Chapter 1. A Holy Materialism

1. Denis Goulet, *The Uncertain Promise* (New York, IDOC/North America, 1977).

2. *Renewing the Earth: Catholic Documents on Peace, Justice and Liberation*, ed. by J. O'Brien and Thomas A. Shannon (Garden City: Image Books, 1977); *The Gospel of Peace and Justice*, presented by Joseph Gremillion (Maryknoll: Orbis, 1975).

3. Walbert Buhlman, *The Coming of the Third Church* (Slough, England: St. Paul Publications, 1974), pp. 154-60.

4. For World Council history and organization see A. J. Van der Bent, *The Utopia of World Community* (London: SCM Press, Ltd., 1973). Of particular interest has been the work of the Commission on the Churches' Participation in Development (for example, *To Break the Chains of Oppression*, 1975) and of SODEPAX (a joint venture of the World Council and the Vatican). For a current list of publications, write the World Council of Churches, 150 Route de Ferney, 1211 Geneva 20, Switzerland.

5. Wallis (New York: Harper & Row, 1976); Sider (New York: Paulist, 1977).

6. Teilhard de Chardin, *Science and Christ* (New York: Harper & Row, 1968).

Chapter 2.   Modern Prosperity and the Values That Shape Us

1. *World Development Report, 1979* (Washington, D.C.: World Bank, 1979); P. J. D. Wiles, *The Political Economy of Communism* (Oxford: Basil Blackwell, 1963), pp. 253-71; Lloyd G. Reynolds, *The Three Worlds of Economics* (New Haven and London: Yale, 1971), pp. 31-122.

2. David Morawetz, *Twenty-Five Years of Economic Development 1950 to 1975* (Baltimore and London: The John Hopkins University Press, 1977), pp. 12, 44-58. A few Christian publications (Adam Finnerty, *No More Plastic Jesus* (Maryknoll: Orbis, 1977), pp. 3-5, and Eugenia Smith-Durland, *Voluntary Simplicity* (Jackson, Miss.: Alternatives, 1978), p. 10, have mistakenly claimed that the development of the last decades has been a dismal failure, with the "rich getting richer while the poor got poorer." Although the rich have generally gained more than the poor, the poor are generally better off than they were a generation ago.

3. Donella H. Meadows, *et al.*, *The Limits to Growth* (New York: Universe Books, 1972); E. F. Schumacher, *Small Is Beautiful* (New York: Harper Colophon Books, 1972); Bruce C. Birch and Larry L. Rasmussen, *The Predicament of the Prosperous* (Philadelphia: The Westminster Press, 1978), 34-44; Finnerty, *No More Plastic Jesus;* J. V. Taylor, *Enough Is Enough* (Minneapolis: Augsburg, 1977); *Alternative Celebrations Catalogue,* 4th edition (Bloomington, Indiana: Alternatives, 1978).

4. Schumacher, p. 48.

5. Robert Stobaugh and Daniel Yergin, ed., *Energy Future* (New York: Random House, 1979); Hans H. Landsberg, *et al.*, *Energy: The Next Twenty Years* (Cambridge, Massachusetts: Ballinger, 1979); Wilson Clark, *Energy for Survival* (Garden City, New York: Anchor Books, 1974).

6. Landsberg, *et al.*, 20.

7. Paul Streeten and Shahid Javed Burki, "Basic Needs: Some Issues," *World Development,* 1978, Vol. 6, No. 3, pp. 411-12 (World Bank Reprint Series: No. 53).

8. This approach was pioneered by Max Weber in *The Protestant Ethic and the Spirit of Capitalism* (London: Unwin University Books, 1930) and in other works. John U. Nef discussed the values which underlie modern economic development in *Cultural Foundations of Industrial Civilization* (Cam-

bridge: Cambridge University Press, 1958) and in "Civilization, Industrial Society, and Love" (An occasional paper published by the Center for the Study of Democratic Institutions, Santa Barbara, California, 1961). Barbara Ward started me thinking along these lines with her *The Rich Nations and the Poor Nations* (New York: W. W. Norton, 1962). I found another kindred spirit in Robert Bellah, "Faith Communities Challenge —and are Challenged by—The Changing World Order," *World Faiths and the New World Order,* ed. by Joseph Gremillion and William Ryan (Washington, D.C.: The Interreligious Peace Colloquium, 1978), pp. 148-68.

9. E. J. Hobsbawm's *The Age of Revolution: Europe 1789-1848* (London: Sphere Books, Ltd., 1962), pp. 42-100, suggests an understanding of the French Revolution as the first of the many "modernizing revolutions"—the sudden imposition on French society of changes which had evolved over decades in England.

10. *The Columbia History of the World* (New York: Harper & Row, 1972), p. 844.

11. Anthony D. Smith, *Theories of Nationalism* (London: Duckworth, 1971), pp. 41-150.

12. I heard the phrase from Martin E. Marty in a lecture at Concordia Seminary in Exile, July 1974.

13. Quoted in Will and Ariel Durant, *The Age of Voltaire,* Vol. 9 in *The Story of Civilization* (New York: Simon and Schuster, 1965), p. 775.

14. Karl Marx and Friedrich Engels, "The Manifesto of the Communist Party," in *The Essential Left* (London: Unwin Books, 1960), p. 17.

15. Paulo Friere, *Cultural Action for Freedom* (Cambridge, Mass.: Harvard Educ. Rev.) and *Pedagogy of the Oppressed* (New York: Seabury, 1970).

16. Paul A. Samuelson, "Economics of Discrimination," *Newsweek* (July 10, 1977), and *Economics,* 9th edition (New York: McGraw Hill Book Company, 1973), pp. 787-99.

17. London: Unwin University Books, 1930.

18. Martin E. Marty, *The Righteous Empire: The Protestant Experience in America* (New York: Dial Press, 1970), p. 150; Marquis W. Childs and Douglas Cator, *Ethics in a Business Society* (New York: Harper and Brothers, 1954), p. 138.

19. Peale, *The Power of Positive Thinking* (Englewood Cliffs, New Jersey: Prentice Hall, 1952); Carnegie, *How to Win*

Friends and Influence People (New York: Simon & Schuster, 1936).

Chapter 3. Twisted Affluence

1. In addition to my own reading of the Bible and what I learned from the exegetical faculty at Christ Seminary-Seminex, I have drawn my understanding of biblical teaching on economics from exegetical expositions such as Julio de Santa Ana, *Good News to the Poor* (Geneva: World Council of Churches, 1977); Philip F. Mulhern, O. P., *Dedicated Poverty* (Staten Island: Alba House, 1973), pp. 1-28; and John V. Taylor, *Enough Is Enough* (Minneapolis: Augsburg, 1977), pp. 40-62.

2. Athanasius, "Life of Anthony," *Select Works and Letters,* ed. by Philip Schaff and Henry Wace (Grand Rapids, 1891), pp. 200-16.

3. I learned the phrase from the preaching of William Sloane Coffin.

4. The economic consequences of morality are most systematically laid out in Deuteronomy 28.

5. John and Mary Schramm kept a journal as they moved from antiwar activism in the 1960s to a life of simplicity and nonviolence in the 1970s. It is called *Things That Make for Peace* (Minneapolis: Augsburg, 1976).

6. Finnerty, *No More Plastic Jesus,* p. 200.

7. *Gandhi: Selected Writings,* ed. by Ronald Duncan (New York: Harper & Row, 1972), p. 42. If I have any criticism of the simple living movement, it is that it may have been more successful in getting Americans to adopt more satisfying lifestyles than in getting them to share effectively with the poor.

8. *Does It Matter? Essays on Man's Relation to Materiality* (New York: Random House, 1968), xv.

9. See also Illich's *Celebration of Awareness: A Call for Institutional Revolution* (Garden City, New York: Doubleday and Company, 1969); *Deschooling Society* (New York: Harper and Row, 1971); and *Tools for Conviviality* (Harper and Row, 1973).

10. Gustavo Guitierrez, *A Theology of Liberation* (Maryknoll: Orbis, 1973), pp. 215-50.

11. "The Real Issues of Inflation and Unemployment," *Federal Reserve Readings on Inflation* (New York: Federal Reserve Bank, 1979), p. 18.

12. "Honest Money," *Ibid.*, p. 2.

13. "Maybe I Am Easily Scared," *Atlantic* (December 1978), p. 47.

14. "The Decade Ahead," *Fortune* (October 8, 1979), p. 88.

15. New York: Harper Colophon Books, 1972.

Chapter 4. Integrity in a Broken World

1. Bertrand Russell, *Legitimacy Versus Industrialism 1814-48* (London: Unwin Books, 1965), pp. 79-151.

2. Daniel Bell, "Socialism," *International Encyclopedia of the Social Sciences,* ed. by David L. Sills (New York: The Macmillan Company and the Free Press, 1968), XIV, pp. 506-34.

3. Lloyd G. Reynolds, *The Three Worlds of Economics* (New Haven and London: Yale University Press, 1971), pp. 31-122.

4. Robert E. Lane, "Happiness, Virtue and Justice," *Yale Alumni Magazine: Capitalism and the University* (April, 1978), p. 48.

5. Carmelo Mesa-Lago, "Economic Policies and Growth," *Revolutionary Change in Cuba,* ed. by Carmelo Mesa-Lago (University of Pittsburgh Press, 1973).

6. Based primarily on growth data from *World Tables 1980* (Baltimore and London: The John Hopkins University Press, 1980).

7. *The Poverty Curtain* (New York: Columbia University Press, 1976), pp. 59-76.

8. Alexis de Tocqueville, *The Old Regime and the French Revolution,* trans. Stuart Gilbert (Garden City, New York: Doubleday and Company, Inc., 1955), xiii.

9. *Serving the People with Dialectics* (1972), p. 5.

10. The zero-growth perspective popularized by the Club of Rome books has been loudly echoed in Christian books on economics (Taylor, Sider, Finnerty, Birch and Rasmussen, etc.). This may be partly because limits to growth would put us back in a world more like Bible times. It would become a simpler matter to preach from biblical texts in such books as Amos, Luke, and James.

11. *Summa Theologica,* Q. 94, Art. 2, in *Introduction to St. Thomas Aquinas,* ed. by Anton C. Pegis (New York: The Modern Library, 1945), p. 637.

12. John Kenneth Galbraith, *American Capitalism: The Concept of Countervailing Power* (Boston: Houghton Miffin, 1952).

13. Trevor Beeson, *Discretion and Valour* (Glasgow: William Collins Sons and Co., Ltd. 1974), p. 285.

14. *Seven Great Encyclicals* (New York and Paramus: Paulist Press, 1963).

15. For a summary of liberation theology in context, see Jose Miguez Bonino, *Doing Theology in a Revolutionary Situation* (Philadelphia: Fortress Press, 1975), pp. 1-84.

Chapter 5. One World: Rich and Poor

1. Paul Streeten and Shahid Javed Burki, "Basic Needs: Some Issues," *World Development*, 1978, Vol. 6, No. 3, pp. 411-12 (World Bank Reprint Series: No. 53).

2. *World Tables 1980* (Baltimore and London: The Johns Hopkins University Press, 1980).

3. Morawetz, *Twenty-Five Years of Economic Development* (Baltimore and London: The Johns Hopkins University Press, 1977), pp. 12-22.

4. U.S. State Department data.

5. Anthony D. Smith, *Theories of Nationalism* (London: Duckworth, 1971).

6. *Time* (December 22, 1975) popularized an alternate definition of "Third World." It labeled relatively wealthy countries like the oil-producing nations the Third World, poorer countries the Fourth World, and countries like Bangladesh and Chad the Fifth World. This usage distinguishes among levels of wealth within the less-developed part of the world, but since it is bound to cause some confusion about which "Third World" is under discussion, I will not employ it here.

7. *World Development Report*, 1979, p. 16.

8. Jon Woroneff, *West African Wager: Houphouet Versus Nkrumah* (Scarecrow, 1972).

9. Kenneth D. Kaunda, *Humanism in Zambia and a Guide to Its Implementation, Part II* (Lusaka: Division of National Guidance, Government of the Republic of Zambia, 1974), p. 36.

10. Joao da Veiga Coutinho's preface to Friere, *Cultural Action for Freedom*, p. 11.

11. "Declaration on the Establishment of a New International Economic Order," in Jyoti Shankar Singh, *A New International Economic Order* (New York: Praeger Publishers, 1977), p. 110.

12. A good source of current information on these issues is the Overseas Development Council (1717 Massachusetts Ave-

nue, N.W., Washington, D.C. 20036). Their publications are aimed at policymakers and the educated public. One of their best is their annual update of issues and statistics called *The United States and World Development Agenda.*

13. *The United States and World Development Agenda 1979,* p. 13.

14. Roger D. Hansen, "Major U.S. Options on North-South Relations," *The United States and World Development Agenda 1977,* pp. 21-84.

15. Doris Janzen Longacre, *More-with-Less Cookbook,* (Scottdale, Penn.: Herald Press, 1976), pp. 15-16, 22-23; John and Mary Schramm, *Things That Make for Peace,* pp. 46-48. Both books rightly point beyond change in diet to actions which help the poor.

16. Sider, 175.

17. Mahbub ul Haq, *The Poverty Curtain,* p. 93, stated my position very well: "We should realize that the true magnitude of resource availability is *uncertain* rather than proceed on the conviction that they are definitely finite. Uncertainty calls for taking out reasonable insurance. The *Limits to Growth* prescription was a radical one, amounting to nothing less than telling the patient to live without exposing himself to the very risks of life."

18. This was the conclusion of projections done by Simon Kuznets, *Population, Capital, and Growth* (New York: W. W. Norton and Company, 1973), pp. 44-93, without even taking technological innovation into account.

19. James A. Scherer's *Global Living Here and Now* (New York: Friendship Press, 1974) provides practical suggestions of other ways for individuals, congregations, and denominations to improve the quality of their international contacts.

20. Catholic Relief Services, 1011 First Avenue, New York, NY 10022; CARE, 660 First Avenue, New York, NY 10016; Lutheran World Relief, 360 Park Avenue South, New York, NY 10010; Mennonite Central Committee, 21 South 12th Street, Akron, PA 17501; American Friends Service Committee, 1501 Cherry Street, Philadelphia, PA 19102; Volunteers in Technical Assistance, 3706 Rhode Island Avenue, Mt. Rainier, MD 20822; Maryknoll Missions, Maryknoll, NY 10545; American Lutheran Church, Division for World Mission and Inter-Church Cooperation, 422 S. Fifth St., Minneapolis, MN 55415.

21. "A Biblical Perspective on Stewardship," *The Earth Is*

the Lord's, ed. by Mary Evelyn Jegen and Bruno V. Mano (New York: Paulist Press, 1978), p. 19.

22. John Sommer, *Beyond Charity* (Washington: Overseas Development Council, 1977), p. 7, for voluntary agencies statistic. The *Mission Handbook* (Monrovia, California: Missions Advanced Research and Communications Center, 1976) notes that Protestants spend about $650 million a year for overseas missionary work. Since nearly 90% of U.S. foreign missionary staff are Protestant, total spending by both Roman Catholic and Protestant agencies for overseas mission must be somewhat less than $1 billion.

23. *The United States and World Development 1979,* Annex C, pp. 205-24.

24. *World Development Report,* 1979, p. 9.

Chapter 6.   Evangelism for Development

1. Bellah, "Faith Communities Challenge—and are Challenged by—The Changing World Order," *World Faiths and the New World Order,* ed. by Joseph Gremillion and William Ryan (Washington, D.C.: The Interreligious Peace Colloquim, 1978), pp. 148-68.

2. Robert Ferris Thompson (Yale University, unpublished dissertation).

3. George Gallup, "What Mankind Thinks About Itself," *Reader's Digest* (October, 1976), p. 132.

4. Robert E. Lane, "Happiness, Virtue and Justice," *Yale Alumni Magazine: Capitalism and the University* (April, 1978), p. 48.

5. Staffen Burenstam-Linden, *The Harried Leisure Class* (New York: Columbia University Press, 1970).

6. The term "Abrahamic religions" was coined by Allen Miller, professor at Eden Seminary in St. Louis, Missouri.

7. *World Christian Handbook,* 1962 edition, p. 47, quoted by Stephen Neill, *A History of Christian Missions* (London: Penguin Books, 1964), p. 506.

8. Leo Trep, *Judaism: Development and Life* (Belmont, California: Dickenson Publishing Company, 1966).

9. Clifford Geertz, ed., *Old Societies and New States* (New Dehli: Amerind Publishing Co. Pvt. Ltd., 1971), p. 190.

10. *Ideals and Realities of Islam* (London: George Allen and Unwin Ltd., 1966), p. 95.

11. Wilfred Cantwell Smith, *Islam in Modern History* (New York: The New American Library, 1959), pp. 62-79.

12. For a sympathetic view of primal religion see John V. Taylor, *The Primal Vision* (London: SCM Press, 1963).

13. *Basic Writings of S. Radhakrishnan,* ed. by Robert A. Mc-Dermott (Bombay: Jaico Publishing House, 1970), p. 85.

14. *The Song of God: Bhagavad-Gita,* trans. Swami Prabhavananda and Christopher Isherwood (New York: The New American Library, 1954), p. 42.

15. Quoted by Albert Schweitzer, *Indian Thought and Its Development,* trans. Mrs. C. E. B. Russell (London: Adam and Charles Black, 1951), p. 96.

16. Dhp. 28, from Hajime Nakamura, "The Basic Teachings of Buddhism," *Buddhism in the Modern World,* ed. by Heinrich Dumoulin (New York and London: Collier Macmillan, 1976), p. 20.

17. Ashis Nandy, "The Making and Unmaking of Political Cultures in India," *Daedelus: Post-Traditional Societies* (Winter, 1973), pp. 115-37; Herbert Stroup, *Like a Great River* (New York: Harper and Row, 1972), pp. 34-41.

18. Heinrich Dumoulin, ed., *Buddhism in the Modern World;* essays by S. J. Tambiah and Heinz Bechert in *Daedelus: Post-Traditional Societies,* pp. 55-95.

19. *Analects,* XI: II in *Sources of Chinese Tradition,* ed. by Wm. Theodore de Barry (New York and London: Columbia University Press, 1960), p. 31.

20. Quoted in Nathaniel Peffer, *The Far East* (Ann Arbor: The University of Michigan Press, 1963), p. 53.

21. Lisa Peattie, *View from the Barrio* (Ann Arbor: University of Michigan Press, 1968).

22. David E. Apter, *The Politics of Modernization* (Chicago and London: The University of Chicago Press, 1965), pp. 292-302.

23. David B. Barrett, "AD 2000: 350 Million Christians in Africa," *International Review of Missions,* 59 (1970), pp. 39-53.

24. Excerpt from Rebbman's journal, *Church Missionary Intelligencer* (May, 1849), I, i, p. 19.

25. "A Personal Statement," delivered at the World Conference on Salvation Today in Bangkok on December 30, 1972.

26. Neill, *A History of Christian Mission,* pp. 507-08.

27. Kosuke Kayama, *Waterbuffalo Theology* (London: SCM Press Ltd., 1974).

28. *Celebration of Awareness,* pp. 25-27.

29. Richard John Neuhaus, "Liberation as Program and Promise," Part II, *Currents in Theology and Mission* (June 1975), p. 155.

Chapter 7.   The Spiritual Core

1. "New Religions for Old: A Study of Culture Change in Religion," *Church and Culture in Africa,* ed. Daniel J. Bosch (Pretoria: N. G. Kerk-Boekhandel, 1971), p. 22.

2. The World Bank's approach to urban poverty is outlined in several sector papers which are available from the Publications Unit, World Bank, 1818 H Street, N.W., Washington, D.C. 20433. These include *Sites and Services Projects* (1974) *Housing* (1975), and *Basic Shelter Needs* (forthcoming).

3. The phrase is borrowed from Richard John Neuhaus.

4. The prayer at the end of the last chapter is a Communion hymn from *The Lutheran Book of Worship* (Minneapolis: Augsburg Publishing House; Philadelphia: Board of Publications, The Lutheran Church in America, 1978).

Acknowledgments

I would like to assert that the sole responsibility for this book is mine. In particular, I should disassociate it from the World Bank. *The opinions I express are my own, not necessarily those of the World Bank.*

I also want to acknowledge how much this book owes to other people. Since my main purpose has been to draw together into a coherent whole various aspects of life, such as religion and economics, which are usually viewed in isolation from each other, the scope of the book is necessarily ambitious. I have depended on critical readers from a wide variety of backgrounds and specialists to help me minimize imprecision and superficiality in making generalizations.

My outlook has been broadened by colleagues at the World Bank: Akeel Al Sadi, Ramgopal Agarwala, Sven Burmester, Ann Foltz, Jim Goering, Cornelis Jansen, Gobindram Nankani, Manuel Penalver, Ian Scott, and Roger Sullivan. I have also benefited by sensitive criticism from Bread for the World staff, especially Arthur Simon and Ed Brady. The following friends and relatives also gave me helpful suggestions: Milton Beckmann, Daniel Cattau, Dennis Demmel, Elizabeth Anne Donnelly, Jim Evinger, Howard Jost, Martin Marty, Judith Philapona, David Preisinger, Theodore Roesler, Floyd Schoenhals, Edward Schroeder, Ward Sybouts, and Barbara Truesdale.

This book began with the religious faith and zest for inquiry I learned from my parents. My wife, Janet, lovingly encouraged and endured the writing and rewriting.

For
Further Reading

Beckmann, David M. and Elizabeth Anne Donnelly. *The Overseas List: Opportunities for Living and Working in Developing Countries.* Minneapolis, Augsburg, 1979. Comprehensive, service-oriented catalog.

Bonino, Jose Miguel. *Doing Theology in a Revolutionary Situation.* Fortress, Philadelphia, 1975. Introduction to Latin American liberation theology.

Casaldaliga, Pedro. *I Believe in Justice and Hope.* Notre Dame, Fides/Claretian, 1978. A bishop on the Brazilian frontier notes, in diary form, the devastating effects of advancing capitalism among his people.

Goudzwaard, Bob. *Capitalism and Progress: A Diagnosis of Western Society.* Toronto and Grand Rapids, Wedge and Eerdmans, 1979. Historical review and Christian critique of modern faith in economic progress.

Gremillion, Joseph and William Ryan, ed. *World Faiths and the New World Order.* Interreligious Peace Colloquium, 3700 13th Street, N.E., Washington, D.C. 20017. Moslems, Jews, and Christians discuss directions of the world economy in relation to faith.

North-South: A Program for Survival. (Report of the Independent Commission on International Development Issues under the Chairmanship of Willy Brandt.) Cambridge, Massachusetts, MIT Press, 1980. Probably the decade's most important official document on North-South relations.

Novak, Michael, ed. *Capitalism and Socialism: A Theological Inquiry.* Washington, D.C., American Enterprise Institute, 1979. Provocative, neo-conservative review of underlying value issues.

Sider, Ronald J. *Cry Justice: The Bible on Hunger and Poverty.* Collection of Bible passages about service, poverty, church economics, property, and justice.

Simon, Arthur. *Bread for the World.* New York and Grand Rapids, Paulist and Eerdmans, 1975. Still a fine practical introduction to the range of issues associated with world hunger.

Stobaugh, Robert and Daniel Yergin. *Energy Future: Report of the Energy Project at the Harvard Business School.* New York, Random House, 1979. Sober, but unapocalyptic assessment of energy options.

Taylor, John V. *Enough Is Enough.* Minneapolis, Augsburg, 1977. Excellent, biblically-based critique of consumerist materialism.

Wallis, Jim. *Agenda for Biblical People.* New York, Harper and Row, 1976. Call to radical discipleship, also in economic affairs.

World Development Report, 1980. World Bank, 1818 H Street, N.W., Washington, D.C. 20433. Annual, authoritative summary of world economic issues, focused on problems of the developing countries.